Root Cause Analysis

The Core of Problem Solving and Corrective Action

Also available from ASQ Quality Press:

Root Cause Analysis: Simplified Tools and Techniques, Second Edition
Bjørn Andersen and Tom Fagerhaug

The Quality Toolbox, Second Edition
Nancy R. Tague

The Quality Improvement Handbook, Second Edition
ASQ Quality Management Division and John E. Bauer, Grace L. Duffy,
Russell T. Westcott, editors

Process Improvement Using Six Sigma: A DMAIC Guide
Rama Shankar

*The Certified Manager of Quality/Organizational Excellence Handbook:
Third Edition*
Russell T. Westcott, editor

Mapping Work Processes, Second Edition
Bjørn Andersen, Tom Fagerhaug, Bjørnar Henriksen, and Lars E. Onsøyen

Quality Essentials: A Reference Guide from A to Z
Jack B. ReVelle

*Failure Mode and Effect Analysis: FMEA From Theory to Execution,
Second Edition*
D. H. Stamatis

*Enabling Excellence: The Seven Elements Essential to Achieving
Competitive Advantage*
Timothy A. Pine

Lean Kaizen: A Simplified Approach to Process Improvements
George Alukal and Anthony Manos

*The Path to Profitable Measures: 10 Steps to Feedback That Fuels
Performance*
Mark W. Morgan

To request a complimentary catalog of ASQ Quality Press publications,
call 800-248-1946, or visit our Web site at http://qualitypress.asq.org.

Root Cause Analysis

The Core of Problem Solving and Corrective Action

Duke Okes

ASQ Quality Press
Milwaukee, Wisconsin

American Society for Quality, Quality Press, Milwaukee 53203
© 2009 by Duke Okes
All rights reserved. Published 2009
Printed in the United States of America
18 17 16   10 9

Library of Congress Cataloging-in-Publication Data

Okes, Duke, 1949–.
    Root cause analysis : the core of problem solving and corrective action /
Duke Okes.
        p. cm.
        ISBN 978-0-87389-764-8 (alk. paper)
        1. Problem solving.   2. Decision making.   3. Management.   I. Title.

    HD30.29.O44 2009
    658.4'03—dc22

                                                              2008055044

No part of this book may be reproduced in any form or by any means, electronic,
mechanical, photocopying, recording, or otherwise, without the prior written
permission of the publisher.

Publisher: William A. Tony
Acquisitions Editor: Matt Meinholz
Project Editor: Paul O'Mara
Production Administrator: Randall Benson

ASQ Mission: The American Society for Quality advances individual, organizational, and community excellence worldwide through learning, quality improvement, and knowledge exchange.

Attention Bookstores, Wholesalers, Schools, and Corporations: ASQ Quality
Press books, videotapes, audiotapes, and software are available at quantity
discounts with bulk purchases for business, educational, or instructional use. For
information, please contact ASQ Quality Press at 800-248-1946, or write to ASQ
Quality Press, P.O. Box 3005, Milwaukee, WI 53201-3005.

To place orders or to request a free copy of the ASQ Quality Press Publications
Catalog, including ASQ membership information, call 800-248-1946. Visit our
Web site at www.asq.org or http://www.asq.org/quality-press.

  Printed on acid-free paper

Quality Press
600 N. Plankinton Avenue
Milwaukee, Wisconsin 53203
Call toll free 800-248-1946
Fax 414-272-1734
www.asq.org
http://www.asq.org/quality-press
http://standardsgroup.asq.org
E-mail: authors@asq.org

To Karl, a superb teacher.

Contents

List of Figures and Tables

Preface

Although many organizations have invested considerable time and effort to improve their processes, it isn't unusual to see the same problems popping up over and over. The impacts on customers, end users, employees, profitability, and competitiveness have been well documented in management literature.

One factor making such problems highly visible is the formalized management systems guided by documents such as ISO 9001. They require organizations to collect and analyze data on process performance using audits, internal performance indicators, and customer feedback, and problems identified are to have corrective action taken to prevent recurrence.

Unfortunately, insufficient effort has been placed on providing guidance on how to carry out an effective diagnosis to identify the causes of problems. Organizations often implement what a participant in one of my courses called a "duct tape solution," hoping it will address the problem.

Meanwhile, the risks associated with repeat problems have significantly increased. Not only is there much greater competition in just about any niche, but organizations and individuals who suffer from failures often expect significant monetary compensation. The increase in transparency brought about by the Internet and various social and legal movements also make problems more visible.

So while the identification of problems is more rigorous, the ability to solve them has not necessarily improved at the same rate. Much of the training that is provided is too high level and philosophical, or is focused on creative rather than analytical problem solving. People are not being taught how to think logically and deductively.

This book provides detailed steps for solving problems, focusing more heavily on the analytical process involved in finding the actual causes of problems. It does so using a large number of figures, diagrams, and tools useful for helping make our thinking visible. This increases our ability to see what is truly significant and to better identify errors in our thinking. It is not the intent of the book to teach the tools themselves, as this has been covered well elsewhere. However, methods for using the tools to make better decisions will be presented.

The topic of statistics has intentionally been left out. Although various statistical methodologies are valuable for validating measurement and process variation, making probabilistic decisions about hypothesis validity, and designing and analyzing complex multivariate tests, these are topics beyond the scope of this book due to their extensive nature. The focus of the book is instead on the logic of finding causes—or as often described in training workshops, it is Six Sigma lite: problem solving without all the heavy statistics.

The primary focus is on solving repetitive problems, rather than performing investigations for major incidents/accidents. Most of the terminology used is what readers will hopefully see as everyday language; thus they can also use it for applications in their personal lives. Many of the examples involve situations with which the reader will likely be familiar.

Chapters 1 and 2 provide a solid foundation for understanding what root cause analysis is all about, and Chapters 3–7 provide details on each of the five critical steps necessary for diagnosing problems. Chapters 8 and 9 provide guidance for identifying, selecting, and implementing solutions, and Chapters 10–12 look at the subject matter from other angles. Three appendixes provide additional information to help the reader understand, apply, and learn more about root cause analysis.

It is important for the reader to understand that this book is designed to supplement, not replace, any guidance provided by regulators, customers, or other stakeholders who define requirements for an organization or industry. Also, while many examples are included, they are used only to help demonstrate specific concepts and should not be taken as recommendations for any specific problem situation the reader might face. One philosophical aspect reinforced throughout is that one can use the Pareto concept (the 80/20 rule) during the problem-solving process, thereby better utilizing resources in ways that will give a higher probability of success. However, given the level of risk involved, some organizations or situations may not lend themselves to this approach.

The book focuses primarily on the technical process of root cause analysis, although other issues that can affect the ability of the process to be carried out effectively will be highlighted. And while many examples are used, the data or other factors have typically been normalized or otherwise adjusted to keep original sources anonymous.

I would like to recognize some of the individuals and organizations that have contributed significantly to my knowledge of problem solving, whether through formal training or experience. The first is a high school physics instructor, Al Harper, who embedded a module on logic in the course. Then there were college and continuing-education instructors Hugh Broome and Jim White, who introduced me to statistical quality methods that helped me understand the importance of variation and its sources. As an employee of TRW Automotive I had the opportunity to continually diagnose product, equipment, and process problems—an experience worth millions. One of Dr. Joseph Juran's early books, *Managerial Breakthrough*, also greatly influenced me.

Of course, what really solidified and validated my knowledge was applying and teaching it for numerous organizations, including the government, military, education, manufacturing, health-care, and financial sectors. My thanks to course participants and their organizations for the wide range of examples and their contributions to my learning.

Thanks also to the people at ASQ Quality Press for the opportunity to again publish with them. They really make the process seem easy, although it sometimes doesn't feel that way when I give up a Saturday to work on a chapter.

I encourage readers to contact me with comments or questions on the book, or about workshops based on the book. Go to http://www.aplomet.com.

1

Getting Better Root Cause Analysis

We live in a complex world. People and organizations often don't believe they have the time to perform the in-depth analyses required to solve problems. Instead, they take remedial actions to make the problem less visible and implement a patchwork of ad hoc solutions they hope will prevent recurrence. Then when the problem returns, they get frustrated—and the cycle repeats.

The risks of repeated problems in today's world are significant. Most customers have many potential sources for their purchases, and this competition means firms cannot afford the waste created by resources producing less than adequate results. While viral marketing and the Internet can help make a new product or service an instant hit, rapid communication about problems can just as quickly wipe out a success. And more than a few consumers and legal firms are willing to take advantage of failures to create for themselves a financial bonanza through class action lawsuits.

This is not to say that all problems need to be given the same attention. However, those with a greater potential impact do need to get the appropriate focus. Repeated failures can be interpreted as a lack of due diligence given the knowledge gained over the past century for how to effectively design, produce, and deliver reliable products and services.

THE PROBLEM

According to the International Organization for Standardization (ISO), by the end of 2006 nearly one million certificates had been issued worldwide for compliance to quality management system standards ISO 9001, ISO/TS 16949, and ISO 13485 (2007). While many of these certificates were issued to manufacturing firms, there also exist many other standards and/or guidelines used by other sectors and for other management systems. Some more widely known examples are the ISO 14001 standard for environmental management systems, the standards of the Joint Commission on the Accreditation of Healthcare Organizations (JCAHO), the Capability Maturity Model Integrated (CMMI) and Information Technology Infrastructure Library (ITIL) for information technology, and generally accepted accounting principles (GAAP) for financial accounting.

Such documents provide general descriptions of management systems that allow organizations flexibility for their unique characteristics. An important component of most of the documents is the recognition that systems do occasionally fail, and therefore provision is made to help the organization identify the failures, diagnose their causes, and take action to prevent recurrence.

However, the guidance given for corrective action by the standards (as well as most organizations' internal procedures) is primarily for administrative purposes and thus provides no help for how to perform the diagnosis. Meanwhile, most people have not been trained in root cause analysis.

The author's years of experience in training people in problem solving indicate that using root cause analysis is not a widely held skill. Schools certainly don't teach it, even for professions where it's obviously needed (Groopman 2007). Instead, they describe how to diagnose specific problems related to the technology under study (for example, medical problems if one is studying to be a physician, or computer technologies if one is studying computer science).

However, *root cause analysis* is a generic skill that can be applied to nearly any type of problem. Some people learn it over time from repeated experiences solving problems, but this takes a lot of time and many mistakes are likely to be made along the way before one becomes highly proficient.

THE IMPACT

Some people simply accept problems as part of life, as they appear to be everywhere you look. Here are just a few statistics to indicate the widespread failure of systems:

- A study by the Institute of Medicine estimated that in the United States as many as 98,000 people die each year due to medical errors (Kohn, Corrigan, and Donaldson 1999)

- Wikipedia lists more than 80 accidents or incidents involving commercial flights throughout the world from 2000 to 2007

- According to the National Highway Transportation Safety Administration (NHTSA) Web site, there were more than 50 product recalls announced just during April 2008

- The Food and Drug Administration (FDA) Web site listed more than 130 recalls in the first four months of 2008

While these public numbers are important, equally significant in their own ways are the day-to-day problems consumers and businesspeople must deal with. Maybe it's a hotel room door that doesn't open when the keycard is inserted, an error in a bank statement, a new TV that doesn't work, or a late airplane departure. At the workplace it may be a document that wasn't signed, a computer system that's down, an invoice that was paid twice, or a product that doesn't work but needs to be shipped.

Such problems can cost people their jobs, their life savings, and their lives. They also reduce the trust people have in one another and in our institutions. As people and organizations become more averse to risk, they are less willing to explore and innovate. Yet it is these latter types of activities that have created the technological, economic, and societal breakthroughs that have made the world as advanced and complex as it is today.

APPROACHES TO ROOT CAUSE ANALYSIS

There are many methodologies for conducting root cause analysis. A U.S. Department of Energy (DOE [2003]) guideline lists the following five:

- Events and causal factor analysis—This process is widely used for major, single-event problems, such as a refinery explosion. It uses evidence gathered quickly and methodically to establish a timeline for the activities leading up to the accident. Once the timeline has been established, the causal and contributing factors can be identified.

- Change analysis—This approach is applicable to situations where a system's performance has shifted significantly. It explores changes made in people, equipment, information, and so forth, that may have contributed to the change in performance.

- Barrier analysis—This technique focuses on what controls are in place in the process to either prevent or detect a problem, and which might have failed.

- Management oversight and risk tree analysis—One aspect of this approach is the use of a tree diagram to look at what occurred and why it might have occurred.

- Kepner-Tregoe Problem Solving and Decision Making— This model provides four distinct phases for resolving problems: (1) situation analysis, (2) problem analysis, (3) solution analysis, and (4) potential problem analysis.

There are, of course, overlaps among these five approaches, and the model presented in this book, based on more than 30 years of experience troubleshooting a wide range of problems, incorporates aspects of each. A major focus of the book is to help problem solvers differentiate among the generic steps involved in (1) identifying a problem, (2) performing a diagnosis, (3) selecting and implementing solutions, and (4) leveraging and sustaining results. The major emphasis is placed on *diagnosis*, which at its core is logical, deductive analysis carried out using critical thinking.

One barrier to effective root cause analysis is a lack of logical thinking about cause-and-effect relationships. An example from a television news broadcast makes this point. The anchor stated that there had been an increase in the number of bank robberies during the previous year and attributed it to the fact that there had been an increase in the number of banks. Yet had there not been an increase in the number of bank robbers (or robbery activities), the number of actual robberies would not have been higher. That is, while banks are necessary for bank robberies, they are not sufficient.

Such errors in thinking carry over to problems in technical, organizational, and social arenas. Individuals often focus on what is most visible, who has the deepest pockets, or whatever is the most politically convenient, rather than what will solve the problem. If such lapses in judgment continue to occur, the same problems will, of course, also continue. Just think what it feels like in an organization when everyone knows what the real cause is but no one is willing to speak up.

Of course, as Dr. W. Edwards Deming often said, survival is not mandatory (Lowenthal 2002). Capitalism has a way of weeding out organizations that are less effective, but unfortunately it often takes a long time and causes a lot of pain.

EXISTING PROBLEM-SOLVING MODELS

So how can organizations overcome the lack of guidance in root cause analysis? One way is to provide a model that gives people sufficient details about the discrete mental activities required. However, it is also useful to understand the potential weaknesses of some of the existing models used within organizations.

The ISO 9001 Corrective Action Process

A corrective action procedure is what most organizations provide for employees who must perform root cause analysis and take corrective action. Unfortunately, the procedure tends to mimic the ISO standard by requiring the following: (1) problems are identified and documented, (2) causes are determined, (3) corrective action is taken, and (4) effectiveness of the action is evaluated. While the procedure typically includes a bit more information about who is to oversee and sign off on corrective actions, what forms and databases are to be used to document the diagnosis/actions/results, and the required reporting channels and timing, the procedure usually does not provide any help for how to go about finding causes.

Six Sigma DMAIC

The Define-Measure-Analyze-Improve-Control (DMAIC) model used for Six Sigma process improvement is certainly a good one. It helps an organization make sure that it is working on the right problems, has the right people involved, is considering critical-to-customer measures, is evaluating reliability/stability/capability of the process data, is identifying the most important factors contributing to performance, is changing the process to reduce the impact of those factors, and is maintaining the gains.

The three steps of define, measure, and analyze are excellent for identifying root causes, but a Six Sigma Black Belt who guides project teams through such an analysis typically receives four weeks of training on how to apply the model and the various tools that support it. So just providing such a high-level model to assist the corrective action process would not be adequate, since untrained personnel would have insufficient knowledge of how to follow it.

Other Models

There are, of course, many other problem-solving models available. Plan-Do-Check-Act (PDCA), developed by Dr. Walter Shewhart and communicated and modified by Deming to PDSA (Plan-Do-Study-Act), has been widely used but provides little detail on how to find a root cause. The 8-Discipline (8-D) model, developed by the Ford Motor Company in the 1980s, has been widely adopted by many organizations, and the recent enhanced Global 8-D version is quite good. But again, the raw form (for example, just the list of 8-Ds) does not provide much cognitive guidance.

A PROPOSED MODEL

Due to the demand for root cause analysis training, the author took his 7-step problem-solving model and expanded it to provide more depth in the diagnostic steps. Figure 1.1 is the resulting 10-step model.

The model consists of two major phases: Steps 1–5 are the diagnostic phase (finding the root cause), and Steps 6–10 are the solution phase (fixing the problem). And while the model looks linear, a unique feature is the iterative nature of the five diagnostic steps. Diagnosis of a problem is a drilling-down process

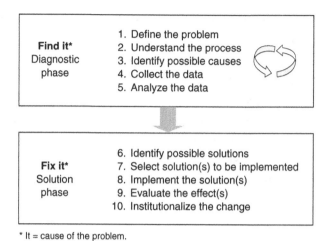

Figure 1.1   The DO IT^2 problem-solving model.

whereby a broad problem definition is continually modified to become a more precise definition that eventually includes the cause. In effect, it mimics the purpose of the 5 whys process, whereby one asks "why" multiple times to eventually get to the cause.

Like most models related to process improvement, the 10-step model also fits with the PDCA/PDSA concept. However, it provides much more depth for developing the Plan, which includes Steps 1–7 of the model. Step 8 is Do, Step 9 is Check, and Step 10 is Act, assuming the expected results were achieved. If not, one simply moves back up the model one step at a time to find where an error was made (for example, implementation failed or the wrong solution was selected).

Figure 1.2 is a visual depiction of the model, where the symbols used demonstrate something about the processes being carried out. For example, Step 1, Steps 4 and 5, and Step 7 require *convergent* thinking, which is taking in information and processing it in a way that makes it more discrete and focused, creating deeper understanding. Steps 2 and 3 and Step 6 require *divergent* thinking, or broadening the perspective of the situa-

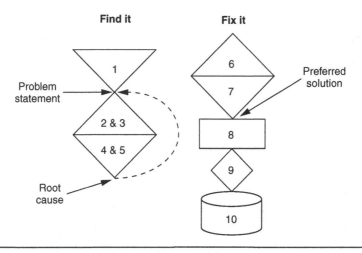

Figure 1.2   Visual depiction of the model.

tion. Step 8 is basically project management (imagine the box containing a Gantt chart), Step 9 is a decision diamond (did the solution work?), and Step 10 is maintaining the improvement and related knowledge.

The model was heavily influenced by the *deductive* process used for applied research in which (1) a problem worth researching is identified, (2) related literature is reviewed and hypotheses are developed for what might cause the problem, and (3) data are collected and analyzed to test each of the theories. Most master's theses and doctoral dissertations follow this model.

The purpose of the 10-step model is to provide very specific instructions that help guide the thinking of individuals who are trying to solve problems. It ensures that solutions are aligned to an actual cause or causes rather than to leaps of faith. Think of it as a rifle approach to problem solving as opposed to a shotgun approach. While a shotgun approach may be appropriate for creative problem solving (for example, you've locked your keys in your car and you just want to resolve the problem), it is not a productive approach for analytical problems, where the right cause must be found and corrected.

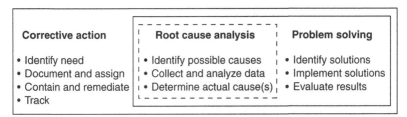

Corrective action	Root cause analysis	Problem solving
• Identify need • Document and assign • Contain and remediate • Track	• Identify possible causes • Collect and analyze data • Determine actual cause(s)	• Identify solutions • Implement solutions • Evaluate results

Figure 1.3   Corrective action, root cause analysis, and problem solving.

Note that the model is not intended to replace an organization's corrective action procedure, since root cause analysis and problem solving are only part of the process (see Figure 1.3). For example, the model does not include containment and remedial actions, which are important components of a corrective action process. However, the model or some derivation of it could be integrated within the corrective action process to significantly enhance the guidance provided.

When to Apply the Model

Experience has shown that the model is very applicable to problems that occur during the structured operation of most organizations. Following are examples of typical situations to which the model should be applied:

- Customer feedback or complaints

- Audit findings, whether internal or external (including audits of quality, environment, finance, IT, and so forth)

- External/field or internal product or process failures

- Equipment problems

- Performance problems as indicated by reviews of organizational or process-level metrics

The model is just as applicable to everyday problems people face at home, such as a problem with a dishwasher or lawn mower—that is, a breakdown of the equipment, not the person. This isn't a book on psychology. Or is it? You decide after you've read it.

All models have limitations, and for this one it may be that it will be less effective in the following situations:

- When technology of the process is new or unknown, which means cause-and-effect relationships are not yet understood. In this case it may be difficult to even know what hypotheses are worth testing.

- When a system is very complex and has a large number of interacting variables, such as is often the case when a major project/program fails. In this case, the number of entities and knowing who did what and when will make it difficult to envision a process to analyze.

- When cause-and-effect relationships are bidirectional and/or nonlinear, such as competitors' responses to one another's marketing efforts. In this case it will be difficult to measure the impact of one factor on another, since they are intermixed.

Adaptations and/or enhancements to the model can likely be done to deal with such issues. Some examples might be using a more inductive research approach (collecting data before forming theories), using causal loop diagrams or system dynamics modeling, and/or using multivariate statistics.

Root cause analysis is a way to react to problems that occur. Providing guidance for diagnosing and solving problems will then help improve the corrective action process in many organizations, assuming there is the will to take on the problems and the commitment of time and resources to allow the efforts to succeed.

2

Multiple Causes and Types of Action

Corrective action is the overall process involved with taking an identified problem and seeing that appropriate action is taken to resolve it. Within the corrective action process is a problem-solving process that finds and corrects the cause(s). The problem-solving process includes both a diagnostic phase and a solution phase, and it is the former that involves root cause analysis.

If one reviews corrective action requests that have been closed out in organizations, it is not unusual to find that there is not effective alignment of the problem, the cause, and the solution, which means the organization has simply wasted resources and will likely see recurrence of the problem. One of the reasons this occurs is people often don't know the difference between symptoms and causes of problems.

INITIAL PROBLEM RESPONSE

Problem Symptoms

Symptoms of a problem are the signals that something is wrong. It might be receiving the wrong item from an online bookstore or landing at the airport too late to make a connecting flight. Dealing with symptoms is an important part of problem solving.

For example, the online bookstore might see whether there are other orders in the queue to be shipped that are also incorrect and stop shipment, as well as check some recent shipments to determine whether the same problem occurred with any of them. The airline will hopefully identify and notify all passengers who have missed their connections that some action is forthcoming. This type of action is called *containment*, in that it identifies and quarantines (although not necessarily in a physical sense) all items affected by the problem.

The next action taken is also intended to deal with problem symptoms and is called *remedial* action (ISO 9000 uses the term "corrective"). This is action taken to get rid of the symptoms, such as by reworking, repairing, or replacing the items. If the online bookstore finds other shipment errors, it will replace the incorrect products with correct ones. Airlines will often rebook passengers on the next flight or refund the unused portion of the ticket if the passenger elects to take another route.

Note, however, that neither containment nor correction does anything about the *cause* of the problem. Dealing with symptoms does not address the underlying cause of incorrect shipments or late arrivals, and finding causes is a much more complex undertaking due to the multiplicity and types of causes.

THE DIAGNOSIS

Multiple Levels and Types of Causes

When talking about causes of a problem it is useful to think about what the obvious cause might be versus the deeper underlying reason that the cause occurred. In this book the term *physical cause* will be used to define the immediate reason, and *system cause* will be used to explain why the physical cause occurred. Figure 2.1 shows the connections between symptoms, physical causes, and system causes, along with examples of each.

Other terms sometimes used for physical cause are direct cause, immediate cause, and proximate cause, indicating that the

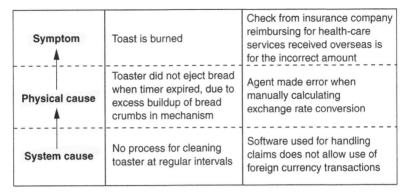

		Check from insurance company reimbursing for health-care services received overseas is for the incorrect amount
Symptom ↑	Toast is burned	
Physical cause ↑	Toaster did not eject bread when timer expired, due to excess buildup of bread crumbs in mechanism	Agent made error when manually calculating exchange rate conversion
System cause	No process for cleaning toaster at regular intervals	Software used for handling claims does not allow use of foreign currency transactions

Figure 2.1   Differentiating between symptoms and causes (physical and system).

cause is often not far from where the problem was found (JCAHO 2005). Other terms sometimes used for system cause are latent cause or distal cause, meaning that they are farther upstream from where the problem was found (Loeb and O'Leary 2004).

Only a system level cause can actually be considered the root cause of a problem, since it is the underlying policy or procedure that needs to be changed to prevent recurrence. However, in many cases one can justify finding and correcting only the physical cause. Digging down to the system cause should be done in cases where the frequency of the failure, the risks or impacts on other parties, and the related costs warrant such a decision.

In actuality there may be multiple levels of physical and/or system causes. Consider the following scenario:

A machine is producing defective parts. It's found that a device on the machine has been damaged, so it is replaced. However, further investigation reveals that the reason the device was damaged was that it had been bumped by a forklift. It was subsequently found that the painted line on the floor that showed forklift navigation areas around the machine had worn off. The organization had no regular process for reviewing the status of the lines and repainting them when needed.

Note that the damaged machine was the immediate physical cause, but this was itself caused by another physical cause (the forklift), and this yet again was caused by another physical cause (the missing lines on the floor). The lack of a process for reviewing and repainting the lines is the system cause. Note that there could even be another system cause that created this error, such as a lack of clearly specifying responsibilities for developing associated policies and procedures within the organization (see Figure 2.2). Each higher-level cause is actually an effect of lower-level causes.

It is sometimes difficult to know whether something should be considered a physical or system cause. One way to think about it is to ask whether the cause could simply be replaced (in the above example, replacing the damaged machine component and repainting the lines) or whether it requires a change in how the organization operates (in the above example, defining who is responsible for line maintenance and developing a process for carrying it out). In the latter case, a policy/procedure is modified, which is usually a good sign that the system level cause was found.

This *drilling down* from symptoms to physical cause to system cause is the same concept as the 5 whys process, whereby

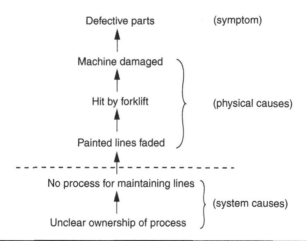

Figure 2.2   Levels of causes for machine problem.

one keeps asking why something happened until the last appropriate level is found where action can and should be taken. If, for example, the answer to the next level is outside the organization's control, then that level of cause cannot be directly addressed by the organization (although it may elect to put in a control barrier to detect and remediate when that level of system again fails). An example might be where a company has been mandated by a customer to purchase a particular product or service from a specific supplier, but the supplier then fails to consistently meet requirements. The company might then put in an additional step to review each delivery from the supplier and correct any problems found. Hopefully the company will also notify the customer of each failure, since costs in the supply chain have been impacted.

Multiple Independent Causes

The reality is that each time "why" is asked at a particular level, there are many possible answers. For example, the reason for incorrect shipments by the online bookstore could be an error in order entry, a problem with a computer algorithm, or a mistake by the person packaging the order. All these could be at the same physical cause level, and in fact, if the organization is trying to reduce the number of recurring shipment errors, it may find that each has occurred at various times.

In such cases the organization must make a decision—should it work on all causes or instead focus on the one(s) having the greatest impact? Simultaneously working on all causes expands the diagnosis and disperses energy, which will require more time and perhaps result in less effective outcomes. The use of what is known as the *Pareto principle* implies that, instead, focusing on the cause that has the highest frequency, cost, or risk provides the quickest result. This doesn't mean the other causes will be ignored, but once the largest cause is eliminated the decision can be made whether to move on to the next largest.

Of course, there are environments where all causes are likely to be dealt with simultaneously, such as when the impact of the failure involves injury, death, or other significant outcomes. All causes may also be pursued in cases where the impact isn't as significant, but where the frequency of causes is more evenly distributed.

Combinations of Causes

In some cases it takes a combination of causes coming together to create the problem. For example, if the bookstore employee pulling the book off the shelf normally uses a barcode reader but can't in this instance because it is broken, then there are two interrelated causes for the incorrect shipment: (1) failure of the barcode reader and (2) the individual manually selecting the incorrect book. In such cases both causes should be considered for corrective action.

Another type of situation involves two interrelated causes, but deciding whether only one or both justifies corrective action depends on the context. Imagine a production line that includes a welding process. If a fire occurs near the line it would be a function of having both sparks from the weld operation and a flammable substance in the same area. But since welding sparks are inherent to the situation, taking action to prevent flammable substances in the area would be more appropriate. However, if instead someone was repairing a metal bracket using a welder temporarily inside a building, it would be expected that flammable substances (for example, paneling or carpeting) might be inherent to that area, and action taken to control the distribution of weld sparks would be more appropriate.

Some organizations use different labels when dealing with combination types of causes by calling some contributing factors and others causal factors (NASA 2003). While causal factors are those that lead directly to a failure, contributing factors are those factors that, when they are present, increase the probability of occurrence. While corrective action for causal factors is usually warranted, corrective action for contributing factors more likely depends on cost/benefit analysis and how much it would reduce the risk of recurrence of the problem.

ACTIONS TO PREVENT FUTURE PROBLEMS

Corrective Action

Root cause analysis is a process of drilling down to find causes of the problem so corrective action can be taken. By definition, corrective action means addressing causes rather than symptoms, but corrective action could be taken at the physical level only or also at the system level, depending on the criticality of the problem as well as frequency, cost, and risk.

While corrective action at the physical level may be appropriate for many problems, if the problem recurs due to the same physical cause, then the system cause should more likely be addressed. Note that while system level causes are considered the root causes, one can always dig deeper. For example, one cartoon on root cause analysis identifies gravity as the cause of patient falls in hospitals (Crossen 2007). While this is certainly scientifically correct, it is likely a bit deeper analysis than is justified, especially because it would be difficult (and inadvisable) to eliminate gravity.

Figure 2.3 is a summary of the different ways multiple causes can occur, as well as how an organization might decide to deal with each. Note that all three can occur within a single problem situation, such as multiple independent physical causes and combination system causes. Differentiating between these can help ensure that actions taken are focused where the more significant risks occur and/or where significant value will be added for the resources invested.

Preventive Action

There are also proactive approaches to problem solving, such as failure mode and effects analysis (FMEA), hazard analysis

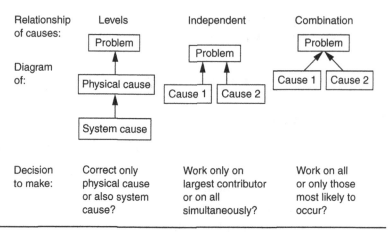

Figure 2.3   Manifestations of multiple causes.

of critical control points (HACCP), computer modeling, and other risk management tools. In ISO 9000 terminology this is called preventive action and is unrelated to problems that have already occurred. Until we are able to design perfect systems, there will still be the need to perform root cause analysis and take corrective action.

THE NEED FOR FILTERS

The need to decide whether to pursue the system cause of problems has been identified. However, this isn't the only filter that organizations need for their corrective action processes. Perhaps most important is whether a particular problem even warrants a diagnosis.

The concept of *corrective action density* is another good way to think about whether to initiate a corrective action request. The idea is for an organization to count the number of corrective actions initiated in a particular period of time and divide this by the number of employees. Imagine an organization with 250 employees having 400 corrective actions within a year.

This means more than one per employee, and given that only a relatively small number of individuals are actually involved in the process, those who carry out corrective actions are likely significantly overloaded. Think about it another way—400 corrective actions in a year is approximately 8 per week.

The basic question is how effective an organization can be at diagnosing problems if employees have multiple corrective actions coming at them while they're already working on several. The answer is obvious: They're unlikely to be able to do a good job on more than a small number.

The answer is to have a filter, along with guidance for its use, that screens problems for whether they warrant an investigation or whether they will instead be entered into a database or other tracking device that allows watching for repeat occurrence. Note that the criteria for the filter are similar to the criteria for physical cause versus system cause: frequency, cost, and risk, plus how many corrective actions are already open. For most organizations the specific numbers can't be predefined, as they will change over time due to changes in products/processes, resource availability, and so forth. Figure 2.4 demonstrates the

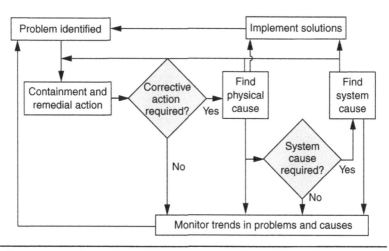

Figure 2.4 Filters for the corrective action process.

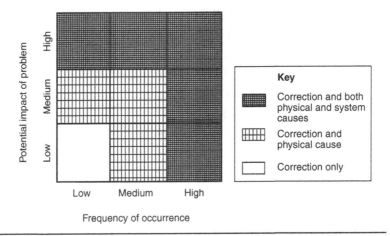

Figure 2.5   Nonconformity risk matrix.

overall corrective action process and where these decisions need to be made; Figure 2.5 is an example of a matrix that might be used to help rank problems in order to make a decision.

3

Step 1: Define the Problem

"A problem well stated is a problem half solved" is a common phrase in the problem-solving field attributed to former GM executive Charles Kettering (Willingham 1999, 162). That is, rather than jumping to conclusions, if we take the time to ensure that we have a clear understanding of what the problem really is (or isn't), it will save a lot of time further on that might have been wasted. Put another way: less chasing of ghosts!

Someone at work has told you that the copier isn't working. Would you tell him to make sure there was paper in the machine? If so, there's a good chance that checking the paper supply would be a waste of his time. Why? There are many other reasons a copier might not work (for example, the scanning light is burned out, the toner is low, the electricity is off, or there is a mechanical feed problem), and his statement of the problem does not point to a lack of paper as being any more likely than any of the other potential causes.

A good problem definition can help make the diagnosis more focused and productive. However, even before defining the problem it is worth considering whether the problem is important enough to work on relative to other issues, as well as whether it is sufficiently narrowly scoped to allow an analysis having a high signal-to-noise ratio. A low signal-to-noise ratio makes if difficult to differentiate between cause-and-effect relationships because of having too broad a focus that includes many similar problems with different causes.

SELECTING THE RIGHT PROBLEM

Earlier it was discussed that there should be a filter before the corrective action process that identifies which problems require action versus those that would simply be trended over time. However, not all problems identified in an organization will go into this filter. For example, if a company begins losing market share, this would typically not be considered as an issue that would be entered into the corrective action process. Yet it is one that might be of great significance to the future of the company, and to which root cause analysis could be applied by creating a task force to investigate it.

So before working on any problem, one must consider how many other issues are facing the organization and which of these justifies reallocation of resources to solve the problem. This requires looking at the relative frequency of the problem, the cost impact, related risks (legal, regulatory, business loss), and opportunity costs (how well does it fit with future strategic direction, are there sufficient resources available to work on it, and for what else could those resources be used).

Note that even though a problem might have minimal risks or direct cost, if it occurs at a high frequency it may disrupt the organization in ways that are more troublesome than immediately apparent. For example, it might cause a reduction in capacity, which could begin to affect on-time delivery or the ability to take on new business.

Table 3.1   Project decision matrix.

Potential project	Customer impact	Image	Speed	Cost	Total
Wrong food delivered to table	9	9	9	3	30
High waitstaff turnover	1	3	3	3	10
Insufficient seating	3	3	3	3	12
Low health-inspection scores	9	9	1	1	20

Low = 1, medium = 3, high = 9.

One of two tools is likely to be useful for deciding which issues justify the allocation of resources to conduct a root cause analysis. The first is a *decision table* or matrix (see Table 3.1), often called portfolio analysis in Six Sigma project selection. This tool is especially useful when the potential projects are significantly different from one another contextually, or when it is difficult to discretely quantify some of the evaluation parameters.

The second tool that can be used to evaluate potential projects is the *Pareto diagram* (based on the Pareto principle or the 80/20 rule). It is a simpler analysis that can be applied when all the problems are in the same context. However, multiple Paretos (or *pivot table* analysis) will still be necessary in order to look at the problem from different angles.

Table 3.2 is an example of data an organization might have. Since the organization has already decided that reducing scrap is its number one priority, all the data are within the same context. However, it may not make sense to try to reduce it everywhere simultaneously, but to instead look for where the problem is greatest.

Table 3.2   Scrap analysis data for first quarter.

Department	Machine	Shift	P/N	# of parts	$
A	101	1	X	20	100
A	101	2	X	15	75
A	101	1	Y	5	100
A	102	2	X	12	60
A	102	1	X	25	125
A	102	2	Y	2	80
B	103	1	X	23	230
B	103	2	Y	6	300
B	103	1	X	4	40
B	103	2	X	20	200
B	103	1	X	30	300
B	103	2	Y	5	250
C	104	1	Y	2	200
C	104	2	Y	5	500
C	104	1	X	12	240
C	104	2	X	13	260
D	105	1	X	11	110
D	106	2	Y	5	1000

Figure 3.1 shows multiple Pareto diagrams looking at the data by number of parts scrapped and the total dollars scrapped by department and part number (P/N). The graphs indicate that department B is the highest contributor, but not by a wide margin by either number of parts or dollars. However, when looking at the data by P/N, part X is the greater contributor by number of parts, and part Y is the greater contributor if looking at dollars.

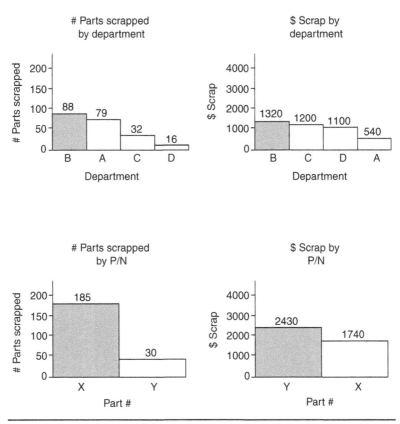

Figure 3.1   Scrap analysis using Paretos.

The organization needs to make a decision on where to focus by asking what is more important. For example, if it is under heavy cost pressures, then working on reducing scrap for part Y would be a good area, but if capacity constraints are more relevant, then perhaps part X would be a better focus.

Pivot tables can show the same thing in fewer steps (see Figure 3.2). Note that while it is still clear that the organization must decide between number of parts and dollars, the pivot tables help show which departments contribute the most to each.

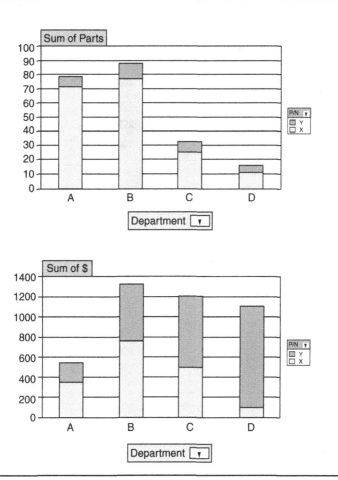

Figure 3.2   Scrap analysis using pivot tables.

When doing Pareto analysis, care must be taken relative to the groups into which the data are categorized. Breaking down a category or combining categories can cause a shift in priorities (see Figure 3.3 for analysis of customer complaint information for a convenience store chain). It is therefore useful to look at the data in different ways in order to make the best decision.

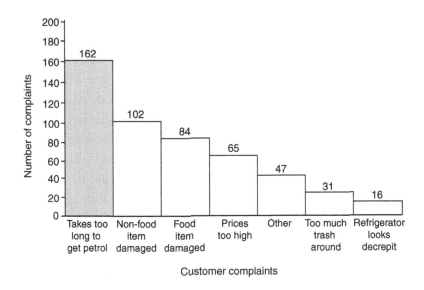

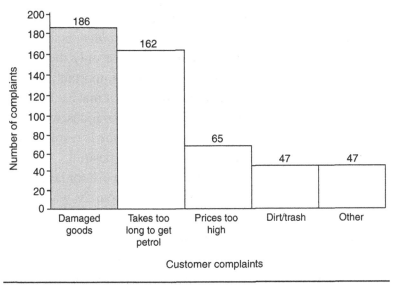

Figure 3.3   Effect of Pareto categories.

SCOPING THE PROBLEM APPROPRIATELY

The difference between departments in the previous example points out another issue for consideration. After a problem has been identified as significant enough to work on, there is still the matter of whether it has been well scoped. Let's take a simple example such as a labeling problem. If an organization has identified numerous labeling issues over several months and decides to work on them, consideration should be given to whether it is really a single problem or perhaps multiple problems. For example, the labeling problem might consist of labels being placed at incorrect locations on product, the wrong labels being placed on products, the label content being inaccurate, and so forth. Although all these may fall into the same larger problem category of a labeling problem, they are likely different problems with different causes. For example, the label may be printed at one location/time during the process but attached at a later location/time and by different people.

In this case the concept of *scoping the problem* is to decide whether to work on all the labeling issues or only the largest one. This isn't to say that each of them isn't important, but that if by working on all of them simultaneously it makes the problem more complex, then perhaps a narrower focus would be useful. Once the most significant labeling issue is resolved, the organization can move on to the next one, if desired.

So again, the Pareto principle comes into use for helping to define the problem. It helps focus energy/resources where they would be better spent, and reduces the signal-to-noise ratio that will be encountered during the diagnosis. For the scrap problem earlier, perhaps identifying a particular reason for scrap (for example, setup parts, destructive testing parts, and visual vs. machined defects) would be useful.

In some cases an organization may start with a broad problem statement and narrow it down as the diagnosis progresses.

In other cases it may first identify a general problem and then immediately jump to Steps 4 and 5 of the model in order to collect and analyze data that help narrow it down to something more manageable.

THE PROBLEM STATEMENT

Components of the Statement

Once the specific problem to work on has been identified, a clear, concise, and complete problem statement should be developed. Components of a good problem statement include the following:

- *What*: A description of what happened (that shouldn't have) or didn't happen (that should have), or what happened that the organization would like to see happen again, or simply what change in performance is desired.

- *Where*: Where specifically the problem was found. Note that this could be geographic, and/or where in the process, and/or location on the product.

- *Who*: If the problem directly affects an individual or group of people, "who" often becomes an expansion of, or replacement for, "where."

- *When*: When the problem was first found and/or when it began (if known).

- *How much*: The frequency and/or magnitude of the problem. Numbers provided should be absolute values (plus percentages if useful for normalizing the data).

Some of these components can also be combined to include more specific information about trends or cycles in which the problem does or does not occur. A *time-oriented graph* such as a run chart or control chart should be used to assist in defining the "when" and "how much." Such charts allow seeing how the problem or process has performed over some past period of time, and in many cases can help quickly identify or eliminate several possible causes.

Figure 3.4 shows three run charts, each demonstrating a different pattern of variation. Consider how the cause for each pattern is likely to be different, with example A being related to something that occurred but then quickly disappeared, example B being something that slowly drifted, and example C being something that shifted then shifted back after some longer period of time. Such analyses of the problem over time may help confirm or rule out several potential causes quite early.

The run chart can also help define the baseline performance that can be used at Step 9 of the model, comparing before-versus-after implementation results. However, as mentioned earlier, in some cases this level of information may not be immediately available, calling for skipping to Steps 4 and 5 in order to get the data before completing Step 1.

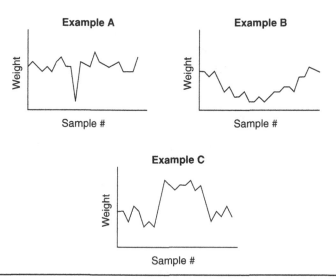

Figure 3.4   Using run charts to inform the problem statement.

Following are some example problem statements and comments on each:

- *Computer downtime is too high.* Although this may signify that someone believes there is a problem, it is certainly not sufficient to allow anyone to begin a diagnosis. Which computer(s)? Located where? How long has it been too high? How high is it? What is an acceptable level of downtime, or what was the level before it became unacceptable? What type of downtime (for example, breakdown, software upgrades, or hardware maintenance) is included or excluded in the numbers?

- *The percentage of customers whose vehicles were not ready for pickup when promised has increased in the past three months.* How much has it increased? What was the average number per week before, and what is it now? Was it a sudden or gradual increase? Can the customers be more narrowly identified as to perhaps the type of work they were having done?

- *Only 45 percent of fourth graders meet the standardized test requirements.* At what schools? All classrooms or only some (if more than one at the school)? Is it only for the latest test, or was it also true for the previous one(s)? For which subjects (for example, reading, writing, or math) did they not meet the requirements? How many fourth-grade students at the school(s) took the test?

- *Mary, who herds her sheep in Barry, lost three lambs to illness this year. In the past five years she had lost none.* OK, perhaps not the beginning of a good fairy tale, but at least a more complete problem statement. We know where to find Mary, we know the problem she has, and we know the magnitude and timing. We can begin our diagnosis.

Some organizations also include an *impact statement* as part of the problem definition. The statement might specify the actual or potential costs, risks, and so forth, associated with the problem, helping individuals involved to better understand the importance of the project.

Note that the problem statement does not necessarily have to be a single sentence. One could perhaps improve problem understanding and root cause analysis in many organizations just by having a fill-in-the-blank format for defining the problem on the corrective action form. Often information comes back from a remote location and is neither accurate nor complete when it gets to the individual who must perform the analysis. Think about the difficulties encountered when a field salesperson hears about a problem, and the subsequent energy often required by internal personnel to get the details. If the organization had a standard way of capturing problem information, diagnoses could begin much quicker.

Problem statements are often quite broad at the beginning, until either the problem has been better scoped or sufficient information has been obtained to allow a more finite description. However, by cycling through the five diagnostic steps, one is continually making the statement more and more definitive, until it actually includes the cause(s) of the problem. Note that this does not mean the original problem statement is actually rewritten each time, but instead that understanding of the problem is now deeper.

Cautions on Problem Statements

It is also important to ensure that the terminology used in the problem statement is not unclear, ambiguous, oblique, or fuzzy. This can be done by using terminology that is well recognized in the organization. However, the same terms might stand for different things depending on the functional perspective of the user, so a better approach is to provide an *opera-*

tional definition for terms that might easily be misunderstood or misinterpreted.

Two hospitals were comparing the length of stay for patients undergoing knee replacement surgery. Each hospital flowcharted its process at a high level and then collected data in order to learn how long each of the major steps took. It was found that one hospital took significantly less time in the operating room (OR) than the other hospital, which appeared to be a good area for improvement for the second hospital. However, it was found that each hospital measured OR time—when the clock was started and when it was stopped— differently; that is, they had different operational definitions (no, that is not a pun) for OR time.

Some advocate using the comparative thinking process of the is/is-not analysis, propounded by Kepner and Tregoe (1981), as part of defining the problem. Although this could be useful (and is, in fact, shown as part of Step 1 in the form in Appendix B), one must be careful, since the "nots" may just be "not yet." Forming conclusions too early in the process can cause the diagnosis to go down a path based on faulty perception. The author prefers to leave this technique for Step 5 to analyze all the data collected to get a broader view of possible causes.

What needs to be excluded from the problem definition is anything that specifies or even implies what the cause is, such as how or why the problem occurred. Such information is likely to be premature or inaccurate and, again, cause the diagnosis to go in a wrong direction. After all, if the cause is known, why even do a diagnosis? Just implement the solution. But this is precisely why some companies' corrective action processes fail: They think they already know the cause, and in many cases the solution.

An organization was using dangerous equipment that repeatedly failed. Its problem statement said something like "accidental . . . ," and the diagnosis (and solutions) went on for months without achieving the desired results. Only when the organization found out that its assumptions were incorrect (the actions were intentional, not accidental) was it able to move forward with a deeper analysis as to the causes.

Caution is also warranted when including "who" in the problem statement. Often, people point to the individuals or the group who produced the output as part of the problem definition. In effect, they believe they know what the cause is at some level. If the diagnosis is constrained by this, actual causes might be missed.

The final comment on problem statements has to do with audit findings. Many audits of management systems (for example, ISO 9001) are based on relatively small sample sizes, and when a nonconformity is found it is recorded and reported. An example might be, "Company policy requires that all personnel using statistical process control (SPC) be trained in its use. Two associates in the machining department are using SPC but have not been trained."

Note that since auditors do not typically go back and find when the problem began, or increase the sample size significantly in order to define the degree of the problem with any statistical confidence, the audit nonconformity is not a complete problem statement but instead just a list of symptoms. An exception is for financial auditors, and perhaps any others who tend to use statistically based sample sizes for testing the management system. In such cases the findings are typically quite in-depth, and in fact, the auditors often look for the management control that has failed (that is, the physical cause of the problem).

4

Step 2: Understand the Process

One major step many organizations fail to take in their problem diagnosis is a review of the processes that could have failed. Instead, quick intuitive (but as we'll uncover later, often biased) decisions are made about where the problem was most likely created. This causes many other potential causes to not even be considered.

Understanding the process is all about stepping back and taking a broad view of the problem before jumping to possible causes. This is especially useful if the problem was thought to have been previously solved but has since recurred.

SETTING PROCESS BOUNDARIES

To begin understanding the process, a set of *boundaries* for the diagnosis first needs to be established. The ending boundary is usually pretty easy to identify—it's where the problem was found. The beginning boundary is somewhat more difficult, but here are a couple of recommendations:

- Keep it internal to your organization, focusing on those processes over which you have direct control. It is always tempting to point the finger at someone else, such as an internal or external supplier, or to try to analyze the entire system. However, it is better to first keep the analysis to a narrower set of boundaries where the information to be dealt with is more readily available and the process steps are better understood. If it is found that the supplier may be at fault, this also provides useful leverage, since the organization will be able to present information to the supplier about the internal analysis that was performed and how it indicated that the problem was likely caused externally.

- What's logical from a relative process timing perspective? Some processes occur dozens, hundreds, or thousands of times a day, while others may be carried out considerably less frequently. Discovering when the problem started may help identify whether only the more frequent processes should be investigated or if the investigation should expand to other processes (see Figure 4.1).

One must always keep in mind that the boundaries are being set in order to help limit the scope of the analysis, but flexibility is important. If information becomes available that indicates the boundaries need to be expanded, then doing so makes sense. Of

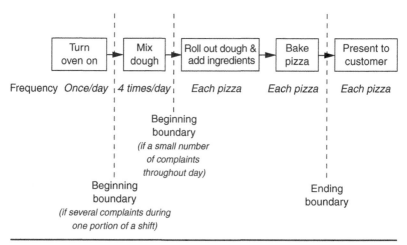

Figure 4.1   Setting boundaries for pizza taste problem.

course, it is hoped that the boundaries will continually be narrowed until the only thing between them is the cause. But if the cause isn't between the boundaries in use, then by definition there's a high chance they need to be broadened.

FLOWCHARTING THE PROCESS

Once the boundaries have been set, a *flowchart* can be constructed to understand the steps between them. (Note: Sometimes it is easier to do a quick high-level flowchart and then select what are perceived to be the appropriate or more logical boundaries.) While it may seem that just listing the steps using words would be sufficient, it is important to realize that the human mind deals much better with pictures or symbols (Roam 2008). Thus the list of steps will be better understood if they are inside boxes. It is also important that the words inside the boxes be action oriented (verbs).

Several types of flowcharting techniques can be used:

- A standard high-level flowchart or process map using boxes connected by arrows (see Figure 4.2). Each box stands for a discrete step in the process, with arrows indicating the normal flow of product (whether widgets as in manufacturing, people in a health-care/education/service organization, or information or dollars in a financial firm) through the process. Some people prefer to use standardized flowchart symbols representing specific types of processes (see Figure 4.3), although rectangular boxes are sufficient for most basic applications.

- A *deployment* flowchart, sometimes called a swim lanes flowchart, is similar to the standard flowchart but with boxes placed such that a specific location and/or group associated with that step is apparent (see Figure 4.4).

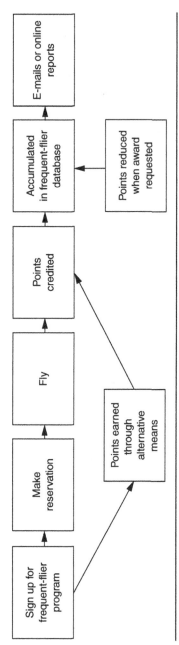

Figure 4.2   Standard process flowchart.

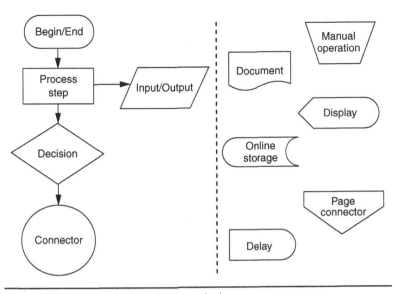

Figure 4.3   Example flowchart symbols.

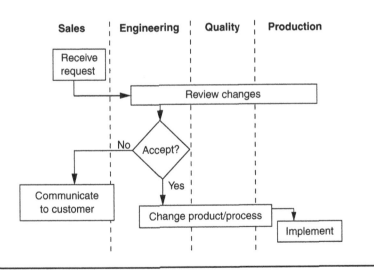

Figure 4.4   Deployment flowchart for an engineering change request.

Many processes won't necessarily be serial, or they may have a loop back from a later step to an earlier one, such as for rework. Some processes are a continual loop, such as a repair depot that returns a repaired product to the user, only to get it back again at a later date if it fails.

In general it is recommended that the flowchart have no fewer than four and no more than eight steps. This allows sufficient understanding of the process without overanalyzing it. Including too much detail will in many cases be a waste of resources/time, especially if several of the steps are able to be ruled out as potential causes of the problem in Step 3.

However, there are times when the flowchart might benefit from more detail, such as when there are parallel paths for the same activity (for example, several airline counter personnel who are simultaneously tagging bags). This level of detail can be of value during Step 4, as it can help show how data will need to be gathered so they can be stratified.

The flowchart is usually the primary process involved in the problem. In reality there are many other administrative/support processes that feed into each step of the process, such as the hiring and training of personnel, and acquisition and maintenance of equipment (see Figure 4.5). While the physical cause is likely to

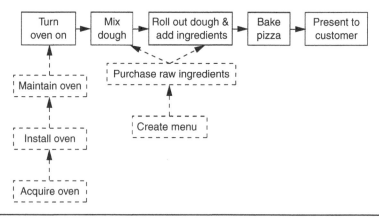

Figure 4.5   Primary versus administrative/support processes.

be found in the primary process, the system cause is likely to be in one of these support processes. But until the physical cause is known, digging into these side processes may be an unproductive random search.

There are also times when there isn't a standardized, documented process that can be flowcharted, since it's just not something that would typically be documented. For example, although organizations implement policies, there is usually no process defined for how to do policy implementation in general. Yet if the organization was trying to diagnose a policy compliance issue, a flowchart could be developed to describe this generic process (see Figure 4.6) and to diagnose where a particular problem may have occurred.

People sometimes have difficulty deciding how to break a process into steps that make sense. The following guidelines are helpful:

- Consider the locations where the process steps are carried out. In many cases it makes sense to have each location be a separate box in the flowchart.

- Consider who is doing the work. If all the work is done in the same general location but portions are done by different people, then having each individual be a separate box in the flowchart might make sense.

- Consider the amount of time each step of the process takes. The flowchart may be more useful if each step is a similar length of time.

Figure 4.6   Generic process for policy development and implementation.

It is likely that some combination of these three guidelines can work for most processes. Company procedures may also be useful when developing the flowchart, as they define how the process is to work. When working on repetitive-type problems it is better to start with this "should be" flowchart, then look at what deviations may have occurred that may have caused the problem. In incident-type problems (see Chapter 11) the reverse is usually done, whereby what actually happened is flowcharted first and then analyzed for how it varied from what should have occurred.

WHY PROCESS IS SO IMPORTANT

Why the focus on process? Because everything we do is a process, often demonstrated by use of the SIPOC (Supplier-Input-Process-Output-Customer) diagram (see Figure 4.7). In a process, there is a prescribed or natural time order in which things get done, where something is transferred from one step to another. When the output of a process isn't satisfactory (that is, the objectives are not being met), something probably went wrong within the process. This generic process thinking can be applied to any type of organization, as shown in Appendix B, Figure B.1.

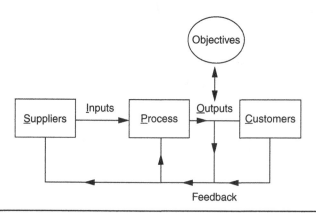

Figure 4.7   SIPOC diagram.

The process being analyzed may be an entire organization, a single facility, a broad business process, or a narrow process within one department or work area. Problems in organizations are therefore the result of failures of one or more of these processes (or an external process that affects the organization).

Here are some reasons processes fail:

- If there are no defined standards for how the process is to be carried out, people will do what they perceive as necessary or sufficient. In many cases they'll be correct, but other times they won't and a problem will occur. This isn't to say that all processes in every organization should be spelled out, as the knowledge and creativity of people should be used when appropriate. However, for critical and highly repetitive processes especially, there should be standards for how to carry them out. The standards might be detailed procedures or work instructions, flowcharts, checklists, or other forms of guidance such as training.

- The process definition is incorrect. One can almost never imagine every possible scenario and address it in a procedure. Therefore, process definitions will be either too specific, not allowing variance for dealing with something that might be encountered, or not specific enough, creating excess variation.

- Sometimes the process definition is not followed. This may be intentional or unintentional. Dealing with necessary workarounds (for example, the process definition may be incorrect) is often found, or perhaps people have been told to deviate for other reasons.

It is important to realize that processes and their related equipment, information, and other resources make up the systems within which people work. So often when a problem occurs, the first question asked is "Who did it?" rather than "Which process failed?" The reality is that it is usually the system that fails to provide a process that is sufficiently robust.

Several new customers of a high-end fitness club have complained that their name on their membership card was misspelled. The owner is likely to caution the desk clerk to be more careful in the future. If the problem continues, the owner may eventually take time to find out why, and learn that the desk clerk has dyslexia.

Are the misspellings occurring because of the clerk or because of a process failure? If the owner had a more effective screening process for hiring, this problem would likely not have occurred. So replacing the clerk deals only with the physical cause and not the system that allowed it to occur.

By concentrating on the process, the focus is taken off people, at least until there is evidence that it is specific to an individual. Even then, a process (the system) is likely to have created the problem. As Sydney Dekker put it, "Instead, find how people's assessments and actions made sense at the time, given the circumstances that surrounded them" (2006, xi).

ADDITIONAL VALUES OF THE FLOWCHART

The flowchart also contributes to problem diagnosis in other ways:

- It can help identify who needs to be involved, directly or indirectly, in the diagnosis. While a core group may develop the initial flowchart, the same people may not have intricate depth of knowledge of each step of the process.

- Since it is likely the process that has failed, the flowchart helps show which steps could have or could not have contributed to the problem. In effect, at Step 3 of the model, the steps of the flowchart become consideration for possible causes.

- The flowchart helps identify *data collection points*, places where certain steps or phases of the process can be evaluated for how well they are working.

The idea is to continually drill down into the process as the diagnosis is done (each time the diagnostic process cycles through the five steps, asking "why"), using the new knowledge to narrow the boundaries more and more (see Figure 4.8) until the cause has been found.

Two cautions to observe when drilling down in a process flowchart:

- Maintain boundary congruence. If a particular step was outside the boundaries at a higher level, it should not be within the boundaries at a lower level of the process analysis. This can cause scope creep, whereby portions of the process that were logically excluded earlier creep back into the analysis due to accident.

- Don't use the same terminology at one level as was used at another. Otherwise, confusion over the differences will likely occur, which may also cause boundary errors and operational definition problems.

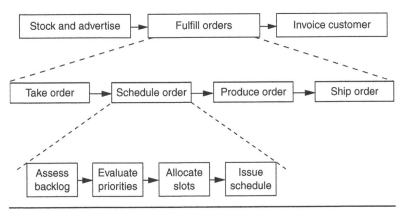

Figure 4.8 Drilling down to find cause.

5

Step 3: Identify Possible Causes

The deductive thinking process involves first developing theories about what is causing a problem, followed by searching out empirical evidence that supports or refutes each theory. Understanding the process (Step 2) provides problem solvers with a broad view of the system that has failed. Step 3 is then about identifying what factors are more or less likely to have caused the problem.

By identifying which factors are more likely, the amount of data to be collected will be reduced, again using the Pareto principle in allocating resources. Of course, it may later be found that some assumptions were wrong and some previous decisions need to be revised. Such is the reality of problem solving.

Three approaches are available for identifying possible causes: (1) treat each step of the flowchart as a possible cause, (2) use a logic tree to identify possible causes at each level of the system, and (3) brainstorm a list of possible causes using a cause-and-effect diagram. It's likely that some combination of them will be best. Since the first two methods are more logical, scientific, and structured than the third, they will be covered first, although the latter may be just as useful for simpler problems. Two additional approaches mentioned earlier, barrier analysis and change analysis, can be integrated within each of the three.

USING THE FLOWCHART FOR CAUSES

Using the steps of the flowchart as possible causes has a couple of advantages. Since it has already been created during Step 2, no extra work is required. Also, if any of the steps in the flowchart can be eliminated, a lot of detailed causes related to that step may be quickly excluded. Thus, the flowchart will provide good leverage in reducing the amount of time and data required.

A copier ejects a blank sheet of paper when you attempt to make a copy. Figure 5.1 is a flowchart of the major steps the machine goes through to make a copy. Since a blank sheet is being ejected, the last step in the flowchart is obviously happening. And in order to eject a blank sheet, the copier must have picked up a blank sheet, so the second step of the flowchart is also working. The fourth step doesn't actually have anything to do with the image itself, other than making it permanent. This means the first step and the third step are the only possible causes.

A downside to using the flowchart is that there may be factors that could cause the problem that do not come to mind when thinking about the steps in the process. For example, environment may not be thought of as relevant for most process steps, but humidity in the area where the process step is carried out might introduce an unknown or unpredicted variable. In order to help surface such tangential issues, the flow-

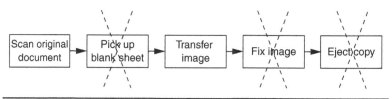

Figure 5.1   Copier process flow.

chart could be developed in more detail (for example, break down the steps thought to be irrelevant before concluding so), or a brainstorming session (covered later in this chapter) could be done.

USING A LOGIC TREE FOR CAUSES

A *logic tree* may be used in place of or in conjunction with a flowchart. For example, if there is no standardized process, then Step 2 of the model might be skipped and a logic tree used in lieu of it. However, the logic tree is the more powerful tool from a cause-and-effect perspective, and it is likely to be used to supplement the flowchart.

A logic tree (also called a *why-why* diagram) is conceptually the same as or similar to a bill-of-material or an organization chart and is a way to document the idea of 5 whys. It is a simplified form of fault-tree analysis, which looks at the different ways a system can fail. It might be thought of as a cause-and-effect diagram on steroids, as it breaks down the system being analyzed into logical, incremental cause-and-effect relationships. One significant advantage of the logic tree is that it allows infinite depth in drilling down into the system being analyzed.

Figure 5.2 is a logic tree for the copier problem discussed earlier. Note that only the steps of the process that could have failed (or technical ways the problem could have occurred) are shown. This is as far as the analysis needs to go, as the most likely causes are the two shown. The diagnosis could then progress to Step 4 of the model in order to collect data to find out which actually did fail. For example, if the image scan light in the first step isn't working, then it could not be scanning properly, and the third step would be eliminated (for now) as a possible cause.

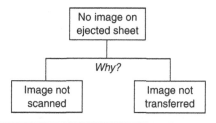

Figure 5.2   Logic tree for copier problem.

Logic trees can break the system down in different ways:

- *Component focused*—Figure 5.3 shows the next level of the logic tree for the copier problem, where the focus is on which component of the copier might have failed.

- *Failure mode focused*—Figure 5.4 shows that there are only two primary ways the frequent-flier account could be wrong.

- *Process focused*—Figure 5.5 shows the three major steps involved in providing a hospital patient with medication; the steps were used as the possible causes at the first level of the logic tree.

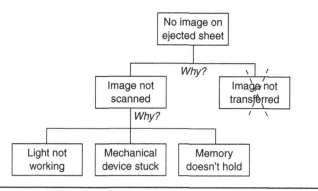

Figure 5.3   Deeper logic tree for copier problem.

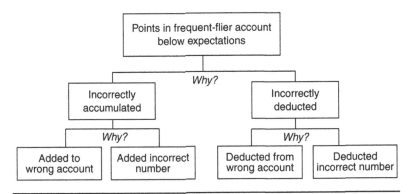

Figure 5.4   Frequent-flier point error.

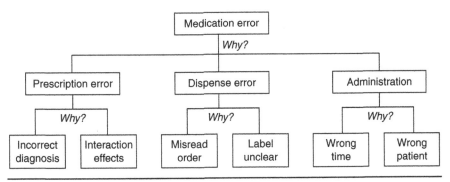

Figure 5.5   Process-focused logic tree.

Two additional logic trees are shown (Figures 5.6 and 5.7) to demonstrate that logic trees can also be used to deal with softer and more complex problem situations. Note that none of these logic trees are complete, in that they do not get down to either the physical cause or the system cause. The tool is simply used each time through the five diagnostic steps, developing it one level further and eliminating as many causes at that level as possible. Another significant advantage of the logic tree is that it automatically leads into system causes if the analysis at that level is desired. When the physical cause has been found, all that is required to continue to the system cause is to add more

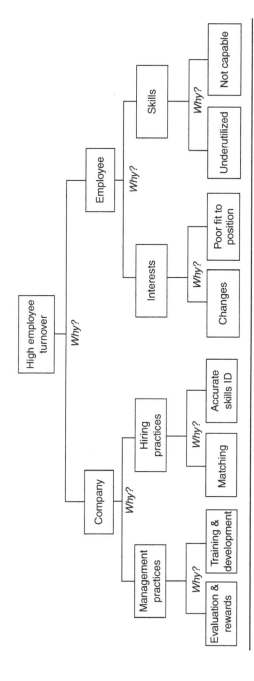

Figure 5.6 Employee voluntary turnover problem.

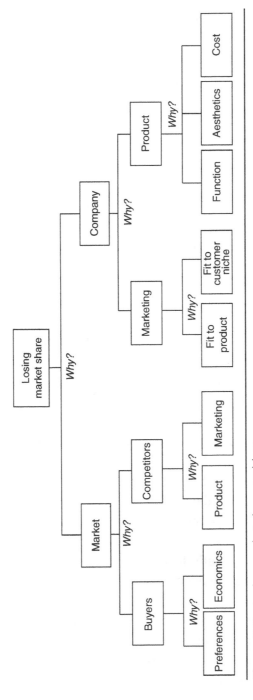

Figure 5.7 Losing market share problem.

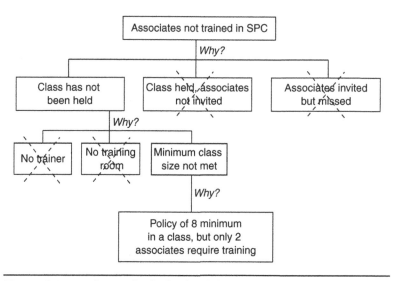

Figure 5.8   Logic tree for lack of training.

levels, asking why the physical cause occurred (see Figure 5.8 for a simple example).

As discussed for flowcharts, the terminology used in logic trees can also be important. The top level of the logic tree should be the problem statement (or some shorter description of the problem symptoms), and each level below that should sufficiently describe the causes. For example, "inadequate training" is better than just "training." Each level of the logic tree is developed by asking why or how the step above could have occurred.

One of the powers of logic trees is that they provide for incremental cause-and-effect analysis, rather than making gigantic leaps of faith. In one of the author's classes, someone once described damaged product as being caused by operator attitudes. Recognizing that an attitude alone cannot damage something (other than one's own mind), the author pushed the class to define how the product could get damaged. Such damage would have to be a function of the laws of physics, chemistry, and so forth.

Flowcharts and logic trees can be used in combination, taking advantage of the power of each. A flowchart gives a time (horizontal) orientation of the problem, while the logic tree gives a structural (vertical) relationship. Each provides a different perspective that allows one to gain a better understanding of the system being analyzed. If a diagnosis comes to a halt when using a flowchart or logic tree, switching to the other at the level of analysis where stuck will often help break the problem open. This draws on both ways the brain processes patterns of information—sequentially and spatially (Hawkins 2004).

One final but important comment on logic trees is useful. Some organizations use a standardized logic tree to help them consistently classify causes of problems. For example, the DOE guideline mentioned in Chapter 1 includes a standard logic tree that DOE facilities must use to code the causes of occurrences. This has the advantage of allowing them to look both within and across facilities for common, repetitive causes and identify more systemic issues. Given that DOE facilities often involve very high-risk processes and substances, they deserve kudos for their efforts.

The downside to the use of a standard logic tree is that the language is not fine-tuned to the specific failure that has occurred. Personnel may therefore find it useful to develop their own logic tree in order to diagnose a particular problem, and then use a standardized logic tree to classify their finding when required.

USING BRAINSTORMING AND THE CAUSE-AND-EFFECT DIAGRAM FOR CAUSES

One of the major advantages of using high-level steps in a flowchart and/or high-level categories in a logic tree as possible causes is that each contains within it many more detailed causes. Therefore, if one or more of the high-level items can be demonstrated as not being the cause, eliminating it from the list also eliminates all the detailed, microlevel causes associated with it.

However, for simple problems, or as a way to supplement other methods for identifying possible causes, *brainstorming* and a *cause-and-effect diagram* may be used, and they are often used in tandem. The cause-and-effect diagram (see Figure 5.9 for a partial cause-and-effect diagram related to a hotel reservation problem) is conceptually the same as a logic tree, although simpler to implement. Of course, with this simplicity comes a few weaknesses, such as lack of room to drill down very far, and items often seem to fit into multiple categories. It is still a useful tool, however, even if it is used just for triggering thoughts during brainstorming.

Typical categories used in the cause-and-effect diagram for manufacturing processes are the seven Ms: manpower (people), methods, material, machinery, measurements, Mother Earth (environment), and management (policies, culture). In an office environment the four Ps are often used: policy, people, procedures, and place (facilities and equipment). Some organizations find it more productive to simply brainstorm a list of causes and then create their own categories by grouping together similar items on the list.

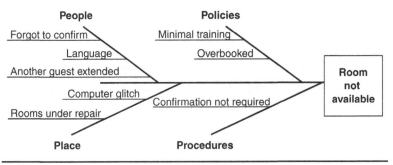

Figure 5.9 Cause-and-effect diagram.

Most people are familiar with the concept of brainstorming but may not be aware of the methods for doing it. Descriptions of four brainstorming approaches follow.

Unstructured Brainstorming

Unstructured brainstorming is the traditional, open, "everyone shout out ideas" approach that gets a good flow of ideas going. The downside is that there may be people in the room who don't normally speak up or who just aren't quick enough to be heard over others. The rule of "no discussions or critiques during the brainstorming session" is critical for keeping the energy and flow high.

Structured Brainstorming

Structured brainstorming begins with one person in the room stating one idea, then the opportunity to contribute rotates either clockwise or counterclockwise to the next person and continues until everyone is out of ideas. If an individual doesn't have an idea, he or she simply says "pass" (for this round only) and the turn moves on to the next person. When everyone says pass on the same round, the session ends. This approach makes sure everyone gets equal time/opportunity, but it obviously chafes folks who are full of ideas. One way to overcome this is to use the unstructured approach first, then follow up with the structured approach to see if anyone else has any ideas.

Round Robin Brainstorming

Round robin brainstorming is similar to the unstructured approach but gives people a more limited scope to work on at a time. For example, post several flip charts around the room and write one of the 7Ms at the top of each. Then have a portion of the group go to each chart and brainstorm on the paper anything they can think of for that category. After a minute or so, or when the energy begins dying down, have everyone rotate clockwise or counterclockwise to the next flip chart. Repeat until all individuals/groups have visited all charts.

Crawford Slip Brainstorming

Have you ever been in a room with a group of individuals who needed to talk about something, but due to either the sensitivity of the topic or the presence of a particular individual you knew the truth wasn't likely to be spoken? This can be overcome by handing out identical sheets of paper and having the individuals write down their ideas (the technique is also known as brainwriting). The facilitator then collects all sheets and copies all items onto the flip chart. If an item is listed by multiple people, it is listed that many times on the chart. This keeps ideas anonymous but allows people to get the information in front of the group.

USING BARRIER ANALYSIS FOR CAUSES

Another technique used to help support finding possible causes is *barrier analysis*. It takes the view that organizations use management controls to prevent and/or detect problems, and that if a problem occurs it is possible that one of these controls has failed. The barriers may be soft (processes) or hard (physical devices).

Prevention barriers are activities performed or design features included when designing a product or a process. They include design reviews, finite element analysis or other computer modeling, validation testing, FMEA, training, and mistake-proofing devices (mechanical, software, and so forth). *Detection barriers* are inspections, reviews, screening processes, or other mistake-proofing devices meant to identify when something has gone wrong.

Barrier analysis can be integrated with the flowcharting process by identifying each step that is or contains a barrier, and seeing these as potential causes (see Figure 5.10). Failures

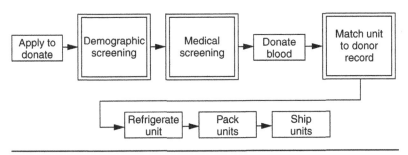

Figure 5.10   Barrier analysis.

of barriers can also be included in the logic tree, brainstorming, or cause-and-effect diagram.

If a detection barrier does fail and results in a problem downstream, the organization should now consider conducting two diagnoses: (1) why the detection barrier failed and (2) what caused the problem in the first place. Many organizations tend to focus only on the first of these, rather than going back to the real cause of the problem.

USING CHANGE ANALYSIS FOR CAUSES

Another technique for identifying possible causes is *change analysis*. It is especially relevant when the problem exhibits a significant shift in performance at some point in time, as indicated by the run chart used in Step 1. The idea is simply to ask what may have changed prior to this shift in performance. Note that it could have been an intentional, planned change or an unintentional or unknown change, and it could have occurred within the organization or somewhere else up the supply chain.

The categories used in the cause-and-effect diagram can be useful here, asking what changes in people, equipment, materials, and so forth, could have caused the problem, and during Step 4, investigate to determine whether any of them have changed. Note that just because one of them may have

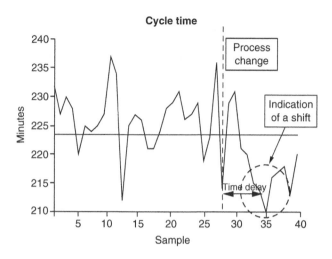

Figure 5.11   Change analysis.

changed does not indicate it is the cause, but it certainly raises it to a higher priority for focus.

A technique useful for determining whether a particular change is likely to have caused the problem is to evaluate the time frame between when the change took place and when the problem was detected (see Figure 5.11). For example, if the effect should have been immediate but the problem did not appear to occur until some significant time later, this reduces the likelihood of it being the cause. Determining the specific amount of time it should have taken to see the effect needs to consider how much work was in the queue between the supposed cause (the change point) and the effect (where the problem was detected).

ELIMINATING POSSIBLE CAUSES

Throughout this chapter several methods have been presented for identifying possible causes. However, it is undesirable to have a long list for which data have to be collected. Regardless of the method used to identify possible causes (whether it's steps in a flowchart, branches of a logic tree, a brainstormed list, and so forth), the list should be narrowed down to what is believed to be most likely worth exploring in greater depth. Here are several ways to do so, in preferred order:

- Ask if it is logically possible (for example, following the laws of physics, chemistry, or other relevant scientific fields) for this particular item to cause this problem. If items can be ruled out using scientific laws, there is no need for further work, assuming there is accurate understanding of the technology.

- Are there data that would allow knowing with high confidence whether this did or did not cause the problem? If so, during Steps 4 and 5 such data will be collected and analyzed.

- If it's uncertain whether data can implicate or rule out a possible cause, or if there is concern that data collection would be time consuming or expensive, another option is to evaluate each item on the basis of the probability of it being the cause. The probability evaluation can be absolute, for example, based on a scale of 0 to 100 percent (how likely it is), or relative, splitting 100 percent among the causes. Those with a higher probability would then be perceived to justify the cost and time for collecting and analyzing data.

SOURCES FOR POSSIBLE CAUSES

By now the reader may be wondering where all the knowledge comes from for the flowchart, the logic tree, the brainstorming, the barriers, and the changes. Here's where:

- From designers of the product or process, who should know the theories behind why it was designed the way it was.

- From those who operate the process or are involved with it on a day-to-day basis and have probably seen a few things the designers didn't consider.

- From those who maintain the product or process, who have probably had to fix it before.

Often, diagnostic guides are available that have been created or used by these personnel. For example, computer models are often used to predict how a system or process will work. Risk management tools such as design and process FMEAs, a HACCP, or a HAZOP (hazard and operability) study are used to predict how a system might fail, what the causes would be, and what the barriers are that should prevent or detect them. For equipment problems there are often diagnostic guides available in the manual or online.

Another option, depending on the cost and risks involved, is to intentionally tamper with the process to see what it takes to create the same problem. While this is not the ideal option, in some cases it is the only way to find out something that is currently not adequately understood about the system. If this option is chosen, adequate controls must be put in place prior to the tests to ensure that there will be no adverse impacts on the people, the system, the organization, and other stakeholders.

6

Step 4: Collect the Data

The use of data for decision making has been emphasized for decades in the field of quality management. For problem solving, a theory of cause and effect is established for which data provide the empirical evidence needed to test it. Note that "data" does not necessarily mean numbers, but any type of information one can evaluate in order to improve the probability of making a good decision. Although the use of data does not guarantee accurate results, it does in most cases reduce uncertainty (Hubbard 2007).

Since data collection and analysis aren't something most people do on a regular basis, there is value in considering whether an expert guide might be useful to oversee the processes. Ideally it would be an applied statistician or someone with extensive experience and training in a wide range of data collection and analysis techniques. Organizations that widely deploy Black Belt or Green Belt Six Sigma training are in effect building a core group of personnel with such skills.

The basic steps for data collection involve the following:

1. Knowing what theories are to be tested; that is, what cause-and-effect relationships are to be evaluated? This is the purpose of Step 3.

2. Knowing what variables are involved and where they can be or should be measured.

3. Knowing what form the data will be in and deciding when and how they should be gathered.

4. Predicting what the data will look like if each factor is or is not the cause, and deciding how they will be analyzed to evaluate the evidence.

5. Preparing for and carrying out the data collection process.

A BASIC CONCEPT

The principle behind data collection is to find what relationships exist (or don't exist) between two variables—X and Y. Y is the parameter described in the problem statement—the outcome of a process. X is a variable believed to affect Y, and there are usually multiple X variables (see Figure 6.1, which the reader may recognize as equivalent to a logic tree).

The data collection process is designed to help sort through the variables to figure out which one has caused the problem. This often involves first figuring out which entity caused the problem and then identifying the state or condition of that entity. For example, if a particular piece of equipment is found to be the cause, what specifically is wrong with the equipment that causes the problem? This sorting through the data involves

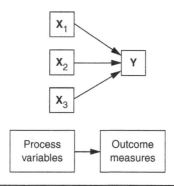

Figure 6.1 *X* and *Y* (cause and effect).

looking at differences or similarities between outcomes according to the process variables of interest.

If there are multiple occurrences of the problem, data can be stratified in different ways to look for patterns that can help raise the probability that a particular factor is or is not the cause. When a problem has only a single occurrence, the association between X and Y may be more difficult to find unless there is only a small number of possible causes or the relationship between the causes and the effect is unique to the specific relevant cause.

TYPES OF DATA

The broadest categories often used to classify data are quantitative versus qualitative. Quantitative data are anything numeric, whether measured or counted, and qualitative data are likely to be something heard (for example, text or other sounds) or observed (for example, behaviors). Qualitative data are sometimes quantified by looking at the frequency or some other magnitude of occurrence (for example, a word, phrase, or activity) in the raw data.

More definitive descriptions of data are as follows:

- *Interval*—Data for which there is a commonly agreed upon natural scale for measurement. The data are continuous in that every possible numeric value (limited by the laws of science only) could exist if it could be measured. Weight is an example, beginning at zero and going to infinity.

- *Ordinal*—Data that have a natural order, such as a son (youngest), a father (older), and a grandfather (oldest). Surveys often use an ordinal scale such as Totally Agree, Somewhat Agree, Neutral, Somewhat Disagree, and Totally Disagree. With ordinal data there is a limited number of points, and the difference between each two consecutive points is not necessarily the same magnitude.

- *Nominal*—Discrete, count data in that each item falls into one mutually exclusive category. Counting the number of chairs in a furniture store and classifying them by the type of material (for example, plastic, metal, or wood) from which the frame was made is an example.

- *Text*—Written or verbal information used to describe something. An example would be asking someone to recall a particular customer interaction that led to a complaint, or reviewing written or computer records that show what work was performed during a medical intervention.

- *Sensory*—Data picked up through the use of the five senses (hearing, smell, taste, sight, and touch). Due to the infinite variety and resulting imprecision within each, classification schemes are often used to categorize the data. For example, color scales for sight, and the categories of bitter, sour, and sweet for taste. Of course, there are sophisticated measuring devices that can more discretely measure some of the same sensory information, but they often cannot detect the subtle combinations that might be interpreted differently by the human mind as it processes sensory data.

Why are these categories important? Because each is a type of data that can be used to analyze a problem in order to determine the cause. For a problem with lawn chairs at consumers' homes collapsing, interval data might be used to measure hardness of the chair frame material, nominal data might be used to evaluate what type of application the chair was being used for (for example, outdoor vs. indoor), and text data might be used to ask customers to describe what they remember hearing just prior to the chair collapsing or while the chair was collapsing. Each provides a different form of information that needs to be planned for if it is to be properly collected and provide useful information.

To figure out what data to collect, one needs to conduct a *thought experiment*—an *if-then analysis*. This is a basic process whereby one imagines something occurring and predicts what the effect will be (Taleb 2007). For example, if one specific possible cause was the actual cause, where would the evidence present itself and what form would it take?

USING EXISTING VERSUS NEW DATA

Some of the data needed may already be available and thus no new data will need to be collected. For example, hardness of the chair frame material may have been measured by the supplier of the material and can be pulled from records. How and where the chair was being used may be included as part of the chair-return process. In such cases there may be no need to collect new data if the information is deemed sufficient.

Sufficiency of the old data will depend on the perceived accuracy, sample size, precision of the measurement, and whether the data cover all possible causes being considered. Records in some situations may not reflect the truth, or the frequency may be insufficient to provide an adequate level of differentiation. In many cases root cause analysis will require collecting data that are not already available, which could be data about the past or new data collected in the future from an ongoing process or special experiment.

WHERE TO COLLECT DATA

When data are to be collected somewhere in a process, a decision needs to be made about the best points for doing so. While each step of the process could be evaluated, this will significantly increase the amount of data that will be gathered, the cost of gathering the data, and so forth. Instead, one or more strategic locations can often be selected. Following are some examples of where data can be collected:

- Where it is already available—This is obviously a no-brainer. If data are already being taken somewhere in the process, simply evaluating them might allow knowing whether the cause is before or after that point. However, it may not be the best point for getting data that are relevant to a specific cause being investigated.

- At the earliest point at which it can answer the question—A problem detected at the output of a process could have been identified sooner in the process stream if measurements had been taken at earlier points. An advantage of taking data at the earliest point where the problem cause could be found allows finding the cause sooner, rather than having to go back and collect more data, which would be required if the data had been collected further downstream. If the problem is not found at this point, the beginning boundary has also been shifted to that point.

- At significant transition points—Throughout a process there are often some points that only slightly modify what is being processed, while at others significant change occurs. These points of significant transition are often good data collection points in that they allow evaluating many upstream potential smaller causes.

- Forward or backward search—If all else fails and the diagnosis will be done by iteratively collecting data at consecutive points in the process until the cause is found, it should be determined whether starting from the beginning of the process and moving downstream or starting at the end of the process and moving upstream will be more beneficial.

SPECIAL TESTS

As stated earlier, it is sometimes necessary to set up a special test whereby one manipulates process variables in order to see the effect. Design of experiments is a broad set of methodologies for helping guide development, execution, and analysis of such tests. However, there are also simple techniques that can be used when the number of variables involved is relatively low and there is a low probability of complex interactions between them. Following are two examples.

Component Swap

Every armchair mechanic has tried a simple version of this at one time or another. This individual figures out what he or she thinks is the cause and then goes to a local parts store and buys a replacement. If the new component put on the auto/mower/dryer works, that's great; if not, other possible causes will need to be considered.

In an organization a little more sophisticated version might be used, especially when there are two or more duplicate processes or systems but only one has the problem. If it is believed that step 2 of the process has failed, then step 2 of the two processes is swapped to see if the failure follows it. If component A of a system is believed to be the cause, it is swapped with component A on a working system to see if that system now fails.

Figure 6.2 demonstrates this for a process application by the dotted lines, which involve taking product from the output

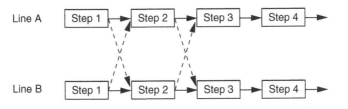

Figure 6.2   Component swap for two identical lines.

of step 1 of each process and adding it to the input of step 2 of the other process, then returning it back to the input of step 3 of the original process after step 2 has processed it. If the problem remains with the original line, then step 2 (and its equipment, people, and so forth) is not the cause.

Multivari

Analyzing variation in a process or system is the core concept of root cause analysis. It essentially asks how much variation does each X variable contribute to Y? The variation may be measured as simply good or bad, or as incremental levels of performance. The *multivari technique* is a graphic way of collecting and analyzing data that allows one to simultaneously see multiple sources of variation and their relative contributions to performance.

Multivari involves measuring something multiple times, but including another source of variation with each subsequent measurement. The sources might simply be the amount of time since the last measurement, a different location of the measurement, or measurement after an additional parameter (potential source of variation) has been added.

A test lab is getting excess variation in its results. The researchers are uncertain whether it is due to variation in sample prep time or the test equipment itself. They tested several samples in which they vary the test time and measure the same sample more than once. Table 6.1 and Figure 6.3 demonstrate the data as well as a multivari plot of the findings for three samples, which shows the sample prep time to be a more significant factor than equipment for variation within the sample. More factors, such as the temperature in the lab or which technician performed the test, could have been added to the study.

Table 6.1 Lab multivari data sheet.

Sample	Prep	Test	Results	Data point
1	1	1	21	1
1	1	2	22	2
1	2	1	25	3
1	2	2	24	4
2	1	1	26	6
2	1	2	26	7
2	2	1	28	8
2	2	2	29	9
3	1	1	23	11
3	1	2	22	12
3	2	1	26	13
3	2	2	26	14

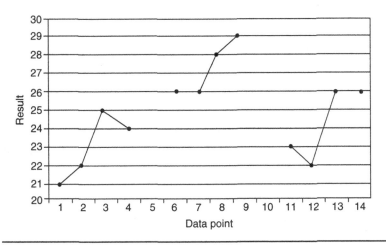

Figure 6.3 Multivari plot for lab.

SAMPLE SIZE AND TIME FRAME

Decisions regarding sample size and time frame need to consider how many samples are necessary in order to provide an adequate level of confidence, as well as when the problem began and how far back the data collection should go before that. Whether this confidence needs to be statistically valid should also be considered. A larger sample size obviously provides a greater level of confidence, but it also increases the cost of data collection.

The time frame should take into account whether there may be structural variation in the process that might be incorrectly interpreted as a special cause. For example, if there is normal cyclical variation, the time frame should be sufficient in order to evaluate it. At a minimum it is recommended that for a problem that has just recently begun, the data collected should go back in time before the start of the problem at least equal to the length of time the problem has been in existence.

In addition to sample size and time frame, a decision must be made about how the samples will be selected. Three primary sampling techniques are available:

- *Random sampling*—Provides an equal opportunity for each possible sample to be selected. It's sort of the equivalent of putting all of the samples into a hat, shaking them up, and pulling out whatever number of samples is desired. Of course, more sophisticated methods are often used, such as a random number generator or a table.

- *Structured sampling*—If the sample needs to ensure there is a more even representation of samples over time, a structured approach might be used. For example, if the population consists of 2000 units and we want to see 200 of them, we might choose every 10th unit as a sample.

- *Stratified sampling*—Often there are subgroups within the population that are not of equal proportion. Pulling a random sample may result in samples of the subgroups that do not represent their proportion of the population. In this case we would divide the sample size into subsets for each of the subgroups and then use either random or structured sampling to pull the samples.

Regardless of sample size, methodology, and time frame, one issue often faced is lack of validity and reliability of the data. Some of this is due to the measurement process itself and can be evaluated. Measurement error involves knowing how much variation in the data collected is due to the robustness of the measurement system.

DATA COLLECTION TOOLS FOR BOTH LOW- AND HIGH-FREQUENCY PROBLEMS

Interviews

Interviews are used for collecting data for a wide variety of purposes. Market research, the hiring process, and management system audits all rely heavily on interviews, as they allow extracting from someone what he or she believes or remembers and how he or she perceives certain situations. The difficulty is that the human mind is both very complex and frail (for example, recall accuracy is often low, and what a person says may be significantly impacted by various filters or biases), so interviews therefore need to be approached carefully if they are to provide accurate information.

One of the best pieces of advice the author has ever received related to interviews was that before beginning the interview, ask the individual to write down what he or she remembers about the situation. This allows a more free flow of information from the brain, unfiltered by the interviewer's questions. Once the written information is gained, it can be used to supplement questions the interviewer plans to ask.

Questions during the early portion of the interview should be broad so as to allow gaining an understanding of context from the other's point of view. Very specific questions can then be asked that probe for more depth where needed. Questions that can be answered yes or no should generally be avoided, since for the most part they do not elicit new information.

Consideration should also be given to who performs the interview. For example, how might the interviewer's knowledge, reputation, organizational role, or personality impact the interviewee? Location of the interview can also impact how relaxed or open the interviewee may be. Initial interviews should involve a single interviewee at a time, in order to prevent the intermixing of each person's memories.

Due to the potential problems with data gained from interviews, it is especially important that the data be validated/verified through triangulation; that is, if the information gained has a particularly strong influence on decisions about causes, what supporting information could be gathered that would help support or deny accuracy of the conclusions? Group interviews may be useful once the individual data have been gathered, allowing an open discussion that can help clarify differences.

Observation

Watching a process or activity is another way to gather data. Again, the potential exists for the data to be skewed, especially if the individual or group is aware of being observed. For this reason the researcher should consider whether to let the individual/group know that the observation will occur and the purpose, or whether more covert means will be used, such as video or observation from a distance (which makes it less obvious).

The viewpoint of the observer can also have an impact on the information gained. Different viewpoints might be related to where observers are physically located, as well as their educational background, experience with the process, and organizational role.

Just as interviews should be planned for, so should process observation. Studying the related standards/requirements, identifying what specific factors are likely to be creating the problem, and developing an organized way to record findings can be useful. By the same token, observers must not constrain their expectations in such a manner as to cause them to miss what isn't being looked for but that may be important. For example, a near miss might be an indicator that the process almost failed but the individual caught and corrected it in time.

Records

In most organizations many types of records are maintained, manually and computerized, which document activities and/or results of activities. One of the reasons for such records is to provide evidence of what occurred, which can obviously be of tremendous value in root cause analysis.

Again, knowing specifically what one is looking for in advance will save time during the records review. For example, what causes are being evaluated and how would they show up in the records? Some of the data may be text and some may be numbers, but as with other data one should take care not to assume that they are necessarily accurate. Instead, look for ways to confirm the data when possible.

Pictograms

The power of visual data for human processing was mentioned earlier. Pictograms (sometimes called concentration diagrams) take advantage of this by creating a visual that allows representing the spatial orientation of problem symptoms. For example, if an elementary school wanted to reduce the number of playground injuries, the principal might create a pictogram representing the

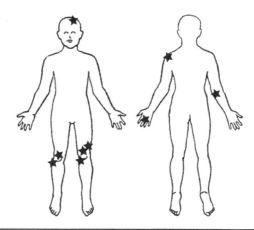

Figure 6.4   Pictogram for injuries.

locations of injuries on the body (see Figure 6.4). Another picto-gram might show where on the playground the accidents occurred. Different symbols, colors, and so forth, can also be used to add more information, such as severity of the injuries.

Scientific Analysis

Examination of physical evidence through the five human senses can often miss important information that can be detected only through more discrete or finite analysis. Techniques such as mag-nification and chemical analysis, along with other scientific test-ing, can often provide a much more detailed understanding of what has occurred. Some of the technologies include ultrasound, elec-tron microscope, X-ray, magnetic resonance imaging, CT scans, ultraviolet lighting, material testing, and computer modeling.

The problem with the lawn chairs collapsing was found to be primarily with the metal chairs. Samples of chairs that have collapsed, as well as some that have held up for a significant amount of time, could be analyzed using metallurgical testing. Some examples might be hard-ness and grain structure of the material, presence of contaminants that could cause the material to weaken, and continuity of welds.

Even time can be magnified through the use of high-speed cameras, which when played back at slower speeds can allow seeing details of very quick actions that can't normally be observed.

ADDITIONAL TOOLS FOR HIGH-FREQUENCY PROBLEMS

Check Sheet

A very simple tool for collecting and collating count data is a check sheet, sometimes also called a tally sheet (see Table 6.2). The concept is to identify categories of what is expected and then record each time the event occurs. Note that a check sheet could also be used during interviews, observations, and reviews of records when expected categories can be clearly identified. A few blank lines that can be filled in with unexpected categories may also be useful.

Multi-Factor Data Collection Sheet

When collecting data on a lot of variables a check sheet will not suffice, so the basic concept of a data collection table needs to be expanded. Like a spreadsheet, a data collection table consists of rows and columns that allow recording different types

Table 6.2 Check sheet for hotel room availability problem.

Room reservation errors—April						
Cause	W1	W2	W3	W4	W5	Total
Overbooked	I		II		II	5
Computer error	II	IIII	III	IIII	III	16
Guest extended		II	I	II	I	6
Room repair		II		I	I	4

Table 6.3   Data collection sheet for insurance overpays.

Claim number	Dollar error	Type of claim	Company of insured	Coverage plan	Processing office

of data. Some columns might be text, others a category, and still others numeric. Each row typically makes up one data set (see Table 6.3).

ORGANIZING THE DATA COLLECTION PROCESS

While the data collection process may seem simple, many failures can occur that can invalidate the data or otherwise make the investment of time and resources less than fruitful. To offset such problems, the data collection plan should be clearly organized so as to reduce the probability of such failures.

One tool for helping organize the process is to develop a table that spells out the data collection plan (see Table 6.4). It could consist of columns such as for what cause the data are being gathered, what are the sources of the data, who will gather the data, what the time frame and sample will be, what the level of precision will be (e.g., how many decimal places), and how the data will be analyzed.

To support the data collection process, forms may need to be created and the appropriate people and equipment prepared. For example, if interviews and/or observations are to be done by more than one person, they should be "calibrated" through

Table 6.4 Data collection plan for playground accidents.

Most likely causes to evaluate	Data source	Sample size	Time frame	Who will collect	How data will be analyzed
Equipment malfunction	Analysis of physical equipment and maintenance record	Each accident when equipment is involved	Accidents for past 6 months	Safety coordinator	Scientific analysis
Ground surface	Accident report	All	Ditto	Safety coordinator	Check sheet
Rough play	Accident report, interviews	All	Ditto	Assistant principal	Contingency table

the use of standardized questions to minimize response variation due to the interviewer. Any measurement equipment to be
used should also be checked for proper calibration.

People and processes from which the data will be collected
may also need to be prepared, depending on whether it is
desired to have the process operate as normal or whether intentional changes are to be introduced. Examples are when there
are certain factors that are intentionally going to be stabilized
or blocked, what traceability information is to be recorded, and
when the data collection will occur.

Control of data should also be considered, whether it is for
identification or traceability purposes, for storage or security,
or for other needs. Note that such control might be needed for
paper records, computer files, photos, physical samples, or in
some cases, even individuals.

Two final notes on data collection, coming from opposite
ends of the spectrum, are worth mentioning. The first is to
always consider the amount of effort and the costs that will
be incurred, and whether the data will be of sufficient value
to warrant it. Sometimes the decision to classify something as
probable or apparent cause is a better option.

The second reminder is to not get more sophisticated than
necessary. A student in a root cause class had a refrigerator that
wasn't working and wanted to pull it out from the wall to see
if it had come unplugged. Her daughter asked, "But Mommy,
why don't you just open the door and see if the light comes
on?" As they say, out of the mouths of babes . . . simplicity, and
in this case a perfect thought experiment.

As stated earlier, data collection is a complex topic and one
that is best learned through practice in a wide range of situations. However, to provide some additional assistance, Table B.1
in Appendix B summarizes the data collection tools mentioned
and shows how to select each based on what type of X variable
one is investigating.

7

Step 5: Analyze the Data

During Step 3 the most likely causes of the problem were identified, and in Step 4 data were collected that could indicate which of the causes did or did not contribute. It is now time to analyze that data to determine which of the causal theories are correct and which are not.

As with data collection, the analysis techniques used will depend on the types of data and the frequency of the problem, which impacts the amount of relevant data available. This chapter describes each of the data analysis tools and ways to interpret what each may show.

The basic steps for data analysis include the following:

1. Being clear about the theory to be tested and the data acquired (during Step 4 of the model) to test it

2. Predicting what the data would look like if the theory were true

3. Analyzing and interpreting the data to see whether they support or deny the theory being tested

4. Considering other conclusions the data might support, other ways to slice the same data, and other data that might confirm or deny the same conclusions

It is important to keep in mind that something can never be proved to be true (Popper 1963), since all possible data are almost never available. However, theories can be proved incorrect with a single, accurate piece of data (Taleb 2007).

TOOLS FOR LOW-FREQUENCY DATA

Flowchart

Flowcharts were discussed in Step 2, so they will not be discussed here from a tool perspective. However, they can be useful for analyzing information received through interviews and observations. Any sequence-oriented information gained can be represented in a flowchart and compared with the flowchart created in Step 2, which represents what should have happened. Any identified differences must then be evaluated as to whether they could create the type of problem being diagnosed (see Figure 7.1 for usual assumptions versus other possibilities).

The flowchart should be analyzed specifically for extra, missing, or duplicated activities, and also for near misses. Looking for differences between flowcharts showing what is done by different people or what is done on different process lines or at different facilities can also be useful if they are believed to be possible causes.

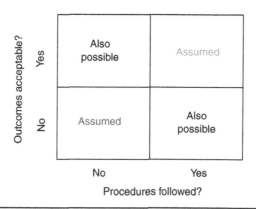

Figure 7.1   Procedure compliance versus results.

Logical/Scientific Analysis

Information gained from interviews can be analyzed for whether it is logical or whether there appear to be unexplained gaps. *Logical analysis* looks at whether it is actually possible, based on the laws of science, for what is said to have occurred to really occur. Data from scientific testing can be analyzed for what they imply may or may not have occurred. For example, if the hardness of the metal chairs is lower than normal, would one expect the chair to fail? This might depend on the specific type of failure found, such as a fracture versus a bend.

G-Chart

A normal run chart involves plotting data at equal time intervals on the *x* axis, and some measured or counted value on the *y* axis. However, if a problem occurs very infrequently, this format doesn't work well. For such situations, run charts can be modified to plot only the point in time at which the problem occurred and the amount of time since the previous occurrence (see Figure 7.2). Reading such a graph is somewhat counterintuitive, but

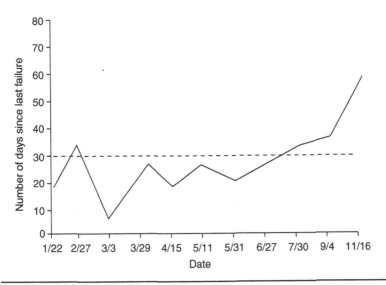

Figure 7.2   G-chart of number of days between failures.

it determines whether the problem is increasing in frequency (a shorter period between occurrences) or decreasing in frequency (a longer period between occurrences).

ADDITIONAL TOOLS FOR HIGH-FREQUENCY DATA

The mechanism that makes high-frequency data analysis so powerful is pattern analysis. In *pattern analysis*, data are stratified into different groups to see how they compare with one another. Stratification can be done by type of problem, time, location, or entity (such as person, equipment, or other potential sources of variation). The purpose is to study variation, looking for relationships or differences that help exclude or point to specific possible causes. Following are some tools that can be used to stratify data.

Pictogram

The nice thing about pictograms is that they not only help collect data, but significantly enhance the ability of the human mind to interpret them. If there are repeated patterns in the pictogram, what does this imply might have occurred? If the data are instead random, what does this imply? What aspects of the process would most likely produce the randomness or patterns?

If the majority of playground injuries are related to knees (Figure 6.4), would this imply equipment failures, uneven ground surfaces, or rough play? One might assume that equipment failures are least likely, since they could cause injuries to any part of the body.

Affinity Diagram and Interrelationship Digraph

If much text or verbal information is gained from interviews, observation, or reviews of records, it can also be analyzed to look for patterns. What words, phrases, concerns, and so forth, were repeatedly heard or seen, and how could they be grouped (using an affinity diagram) to see patterns? Once these groups are identified, their relationships can be analyzed using an inter-relationship digraph. This is done by asking whether improving one would improve each of the others, and if so, an arrow showing the cause-and-effect relationship is added.

These two tools are especially useful for analyzing knowledge-based situations. Figures 7.3 and 7.4 demonstrate their applications for improving the problem-solving process. Figure 7.3 shows the three major categories of needs, while Figure 7.4 shows the relationship between them. It empha-sizes that knowledge of how to solve problems is not suffi-cient if the individual or group is not provided with adequate resources, since resources impacts the other two.

Pareto Diagram

The Pareto diagram was discussed during Step 1, so it will not be discussed here from a tool perspective. From a data analysis

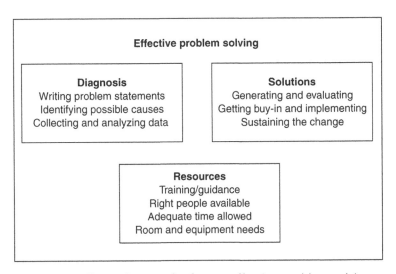

Figure 7.3   Affinity diagram for factors affecting problem-solving effectiveness.

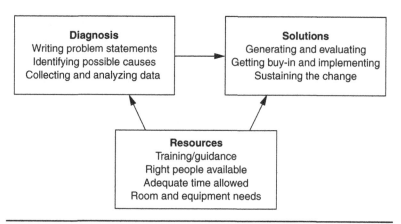

Figure 7.4 Interrelationship digraph for problem-solving effectiveness.

standpoint, it is conceptually similar to the affinity diagram but with the major differences being that the categories are more discrete and the frequency of occurrence for each category is shown. Information collected using a check sheet is a natural for converting to a Pareto diagram (see Figure 7.5, which was developed using the data in Table 6.2). The information can

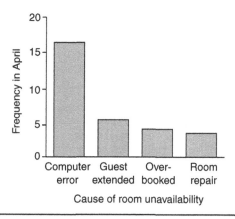

Figure 7.5 Pareto of hotel checklist data.

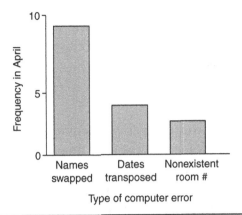

Figure 7.6   Drilling down deeper.

also be further stratified by taking the largest contributor and breaking it down into more detailed categories; this can be seen in Figure 7.6, which shows the type of computer errors that have occurred and the frequency.

Contingency Tables

Tables are a good way to summarize count data and can even help show possible differences and/or correlations between variables. A caution is that the data may need to be normalized (converting to percentages is a typical means of doing so) to ensure that sample size differences or other factors don't cause something to look significant when it really isn't. Table 7.1 is an example of a contingency table comparing two classrooms

Table 7.1   Contingency table: Number of students getting As.

	Subject A	Subject B
Class 1	11	19
Class 2	4	9

in the same school and the same two topics taught in them. The number of students getting As is shown. It appears that Class 1 did better than Class 2 and that both classes did better in Subject B than Subject A.

Run Chart

Run charts are powerful tools for helping identify causes, as they allow looking for patterns over time. Care must be taken on scaling a run chart, as it can either exaggerate or smooth out variation. Typical patterns to look for in a run chart are quick spikes, gradual trends up or down, and shifts that last for a longer period of time, as demonstrated in Figure 7.7 examples A, B, and C, respectively. Some causes are more likely than others to create each of these types of patterns.

Another way to use a run chart is to reorder the data, grouping them by a single factor of interest each time. In Figure 7.8

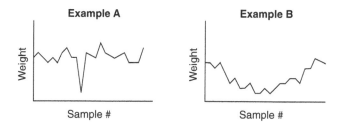

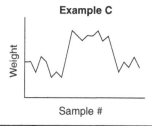

Figure 7.7   Patterns in run charts.

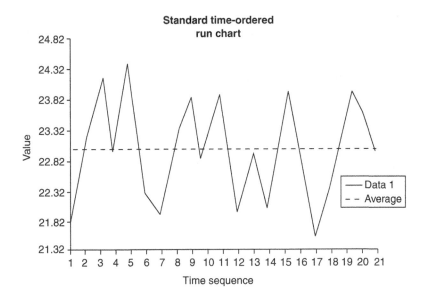

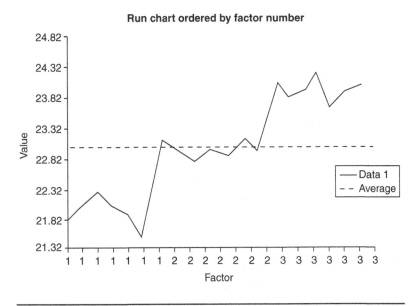

Figure 7.8 Run chart using reordered data.

the data look random when viewed in time order, but when reordered to group all data together for each factor (1, 2, and 3, which could represent different material batch, different agent, and so forth), there are differences between the performance of the three.

Histogram

Another way to evaluate measured data is to look at the distribution of the data using a histogram. This allows determination of the shape of the distribution, and if it appears different than expected, one can theorize and investigate what might have caused the difference. It is often assumed (albeit sometimes incorrectly) that the distribution should be normal (bell-shaped, with a single peak and tailing off on both sides). If the distribution is instead multi-modal, skewed, or contains outliers, questions should be asked. Figure 7.9 demonstrates both a normal distribution and a bi-modal one, with the latter likely indicating that variation in a process variable is actually creating two different distributions.

Pivot Table

The pivot table was described in Chapter 3 as a way to sort through a lot of data to stratify them at multiple levels simultaneously. Not only is it useful for helping to select which problem to work on, but it is also of value when drilling down to the lower levels to identify which causes are more important, especially when the number of factors involved is high.

Scatter Diagram

If instead of looking for differences one is trying to look for relationships between two measured variables, a scatter diagram (a basic X-Y graph; see Figure 7.10) is useful. The amount of correlation (the relationship) is indicated by the degree to

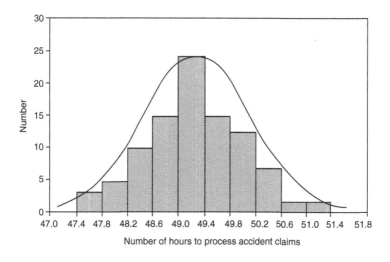

Number of hours to process accident claims

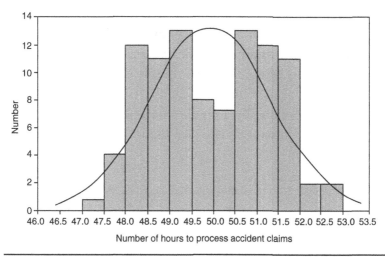

Number of hours to process accident claims

Figure 7.9   Histogram analysis.

which one could draw a straight line through the data with minimal scatter of the data points from that line. It is always worth pointing out that correlation does not indicate a cause-and-effect relationship, but it certainly indicates a higher likelihood of one.

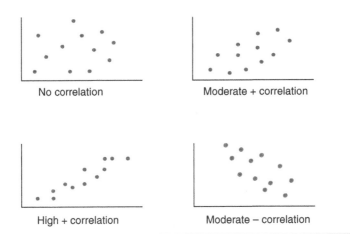

Figure 7.10   Scatter diagrams.

A modified version of an *X-Y* graph can also be used when trying to compare multiple entities where the amount of data for each entity is relatively small. In this case the *x* axis is not a measurement scale; rather, each entity (such as a machine or person) is represented by a number or label on the *x* axis, and the *y* axis is the measured data (see Figure 7.11).

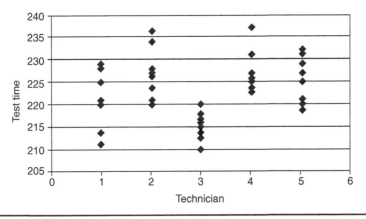

Figure 7.11   Modified scatter diagram.

QUESTIONING THE DATA

Data analysis is all about trying to make sense of the data in a way that explains the cause-and-effect relationship being investigated. However, care must be taken to ensure that the data are reviewed for potential problems, as they might be accidentally or intentionally in error.

There is a tendency to ignore or remove outliers, but they should instead be considered as possible signals that can contribute to learning. Whether they are numbers or text, outliers can indicate errors in the data, other causes not being considered, or the need to collect more data (to see if more "outliers" appear). One simple way to consider outliers is to analyze the data with and without them and see what impact the difference is on the conclusions.

If dealing with a large data set, a good way to question the data is to split them into two groups and then analyze each group separately. The split must not be done in a way that can bias the two groups. If analysis of both groups leads to the same conclusion, one might assume the data to be consistent, but if the conclusions are different, one should question the data set.

On the other end of the spectrum is a caution that if a data set looks too perfect, it may be worth exploring the validity of the source. Making decisions with bad data is no better than making them with no data.

DATA ANALYSES SUMMARIES

Often the diagnosis will involve collecting different types of data from several sources and trying to come to some conclusion as to what it all means. Following are two summary tools that might be used for this purpose.

Table 7.2   Is/Is-not table for packing-line problem.

It is	It is not	Implications
Between 3 & 3:30 p.m.	Mornings, nights	Time specific
Line 3	Lines 1, 2, & 4	Location specific
Sensor #4	Other sensors	Location specific
Sunny day	Cloudy day	Brightness/light

Is/Is-Not Table

The is/is-not table helps users list what is currently known by segregating the information into two categories based on what is found and what is not found but could logically occur (see Table 7.2). Kepner and Tregoe (1981) list identity (what), location (where), timing (when), and magnitude (how much) as the factors to use for this segregation. Once the differences are identified, the implications of each can then be spelled out and conclusions made. The tool is especially useful for complex situations where cause-and-effect relationships are not clearly understood.

Cause Analysis Table

Another way to evaluate several pieces of data is to list, in a table, each of the causes thought most likely, and cross-reference each to the data sources (see Table 7.3). The cross-reference can be coded to indicate whether the data implicate a particular cause, do not implicate it, or could not indicate it (shown as "Y," "N," and "—" in the example). The relative strength of each piece of data could also be weighted on the basis of how valuable it is believed to be. Value could be related to scientific exactness of the cause-and-effect relationship, robustness of the data collection process, sensitivity of the data, and so forth.

Table 7.3 Cause analysis table.

Possible cause	User reports	System error log	Function testing	Stress testing
Software problem (internal)	N	N	N	N
Hardware problem (internal)	—	Y	N	N
User error (external)	N	N	—	—
ISP configuration (external)	—	Y	Y	Y

ANALYZING VARIATION

The basic premise involved in data analysis is to look at the sources of variation (possible causes) in the process in order to find which are present and which are not when the problem occurs. This is done by segregating and stratifying the data to see what differences are apparent. The process is then repeated at each level of analysis as one drills down into the cause-and-effect relationships, and it might occur at levels such as subsystem/process, factor/entity, feature/attribute, and condition/state (see Table 7.4). Of course, some of these levels may repeat as the analysis gets deeper into a complicated system, or there may be fewer levels with a simple problem.

However, what can be seen with visual analysis of data can be impacted by issues such as scaling and resolution of the data analysis graph and the amount of noise/uncertainty/error in the data. For this reason it is useful to verify perceived differences using statistical techniques such as control charts; simple hypothesis tests such as t, F, and chi-square tests; or correlation and regression or more complex multivariate methods such as ANOVA and multiple regression. Such techniques allow establishment of statistical confidence levels for the analysis, which then allows assessing the risks of making an incorrect conclusion.

Table 7.4   Drilling down into problems.

System failure	Car won't start	Medication error
Subsystem/process that failed	Electrical vs. mechanical vs. *fuel*	Prescribe vs. *dispense* vs. administer to patient
Factor/entity that failed	Gasoline vs. air vs. pump vs. line vs. *filter*	Pharmacist vs. computer vs. *bottle* of drug
Feature/attribute that failed	*Ability to pass fuel* vs. ability to block contaminants	Contents vs. *label*
Condition/state that was wrong	*Clogged* vs. distorted	Content accuracy vs. *dosage* accuracy

WHERE TO GO NEXT?

At this point in the diagnostic phase a conclusion should have been made as to which causes are most likely, based on the data. The next step is to decide whether the level of cause that has been identified is one where action can and should be taken, or whether a deeper analysis is warranted; that is, if the physical cause has been found, then going to Step 6 to identify possible solutions is appropriate. If, however, the analysis has only identified what has failed and not why it failed, then returning to Step 1 is likely necessary.

Even if the physical cause has been found and possible causes searched out, consideration should be given to whether the system cause should also be pursued. If the answer is yes, then returning to Step 1 for this second investigation is necessary.

8

Identify and Select Solutions

STEP 6: IDENTIFY POSSIBLE SOLUTIONS

There's a tendency in many organizations to come up with one idea that people think will work and immediately implement it. People tend to believe that doing otherwise wastes time, but what is likely to happen is that the organization misses the opportunity to identify and implement breakthrough ideas, which are likely to be less complex, less expensive, and more effective.

For example, in many organizations the first solution thought of is to add another check step—a review or inspection done to catch the problem sooner if it occurs again. This isn't to say that catching it sooner isn't of value, as it may lower both cost and risk, but it isn't going to prevent the problem, which is the purpose of the corrective action process.

So what is needed is to get people to take a step back from the problem and be more creative. There are many tools and techniques that can support this process. Brainstorming was discussed in Chapter 5, as it relates to identifying possible causes, but it can also be (and is actually more appropriately) used for listing possible solutions.

This chapter contains additional tools that can help the organization see things from a different perspective, improving the likelihood of developing more creative, breakthrough, and permanent solutions. The idea behind all the tools is to help individuals think differently—to see the problem and its causes from different angles—in order to expand the number of options available for evaluation.

Creativity Techniques

Scale Up or Scale Down

The *scale up or scale down* technique involves shifting perspective by thinking of what might be done if the problem were much worse than it is or not nearly as bad as it is. For example, take the current failure rate, multiply it by 1000, and also divide it by 1000, and in each case think of how that might impact what solutions come to mind. Alternatively, the rescaling process can be applied to the physical size of the item being investigated, imagining that the item (whether it is a widget or a piece of paper) is much larger than it really is, and much smaller than it really is. Again, this can trigger different thoughts about what might be done to resolve the issue.

> *Consider the packing-line problem from the previous chapter, where reflection of sunlight caused a sensor on one machine to sometimes shut the machine down. If the problem occurred more frequently (such as daily, or with multiple sensors or machines), the solution might be to switch to a different type of sensor that is not sensitive to sunlight. However, given the relatively low frequency, the solution might instead be to simply put a shade over the window.*
>
> *If the sensor was much larger physically, the organization might choose to put a tubular shade around the pickup lens to shield it from extraneous light sources. Given the actual size, the choice might be to try painting over a portion of the lens to accomplish the same effect.*

Mind Maps

Tony Buzan (1996) is a widely known promoter of using mind maps to display ideas, a technique that has no doubt been around for centuries. The *mind map* is another type of tree diagram that

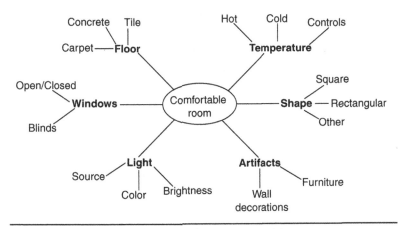

Figure 8.1 Mind map for room-improvement ideas.

starts with a central idea or issue and expands on it, doing so in a starburst pattern that helps engender an expansionary (as opposed to reductionist, as in the case of a logic tree) perspective. Each branch level provides a more detailed view of possibilities (see Figure 8.1).

Analogies

Taking information from one field of knowledge and translating it into another is a fundamental way of expanding one's understanding of a new area. This is often done using metaphors or analogies that take ideas from one contextual situation and see how they could be applied in another. Table 8.1 demonstrates how employees of an organization used analogies to come up with ideas for marketing a gardening tool by using the word "eagle." First they listed some characteristics of an eagle, then these characteristics were applied analogously to the device they were trying to sell.

What Would X Do (WWXD)?

Another way to think differently is to imagine what another individual or an organization might do in a similar situation. It might be a competitor, it might be someone from a different

Table 8.1   Use of analogies for gardening tool marketing problem.

Item (eagle)	Would equate to
Sharp eyes	Reducing the amount of time required to weed
Weightless	Wouldn't be tired after weeding
Air does the work	Very easy to use, doesn't require bending/stooping
Wide view	Can cover a lot of ground
Kill rodents	Gets weeds out by the roots so they don't come back

Source: D. Okes and R. T. Westcott, *The Certified Quality Manager Handbook*, 2nd ed. (Milwaukee, WI: ASQ Quality Press, 2001), 122.

industry that performs a similar activity, or it might even be a randomly selected entity. The idea is to ask, "What would (whoever you select) do if they had this problem?" The idea is to think differently than the organization where the current problem occurs.

Suppose a firm that does security screenings has applicants who frequently misstate on the application form whether they have ever been outside the United States. One might ask what each of the following would do, and then consider the resulting ideas as possible changes to the application process:

- *Immigration or other border security personnel: "Do you have a passport?"*

- *Instructor in a geography class: "Here's a map of the world. Please put an X on each country you have visited."*

- *Your mother: "Where in the world have you been since you dropped out of college?"*

No Limits

One of the problems people face when trying to brainstorm solutions is the automatic but subconscious limits they place on the ideas thought to be viable (see Figure 8.2). For example,

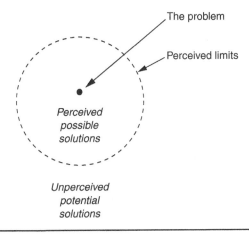

The problem

Perceived limits

Perceived
possible
solutions

Unperceived
potential
solutions

Figure 8.2   Perceived limits to solution space.

most people (except perhaps those in government roles?) know they can't spend a billion dollars to solve the problem, and there are often laws of science (such as physics, chemistry, and human behavior) or regulatory issues that must be dealt with.

But what if those limitations were suspended for a few minutes? What truly outside-the-box ideas might surface? The shift in thinking can be so dramatic that radically different solutions might be developed, and although they may not be feasible, they may be useful for triggering other thoughts or they might be able to be adapted based on the real constraints. The other reason for suspending constraints for a while is that they are sometimes imagined rather than real.

An organization produced a product that was individually identified and traceable, and this information was transferred electronically to the customer location prior to the product being shipped. The product was then boxed (approximately 20 to a container), the box was labeled, and then it was shipped to the customer.

The customer complained about a shipment in which the label on the box did not agree with the contents. When the organization suspended limits, it came up with two potential breakthrough ideas: (1) eliminate the label (which had been necessary before the advent of electronic data transfer but was no longer of high value), and (2) eliminate the box itself and ship the items in a different type of container that can hold more and reduce cost.

Other Solution-Finding Options

There are many other options for identifying possible solutions. Following are some of the more widely known and promoted.

Mistake-Proofing

Also known by the Japanese term "poka-yoke," *mistake-proofing* looks for simple ways to either prevent or warn of problems. Following are some examples from everyday life:

- Many vehicles cannot be put into reverse unless the driver's foot is on the brake. This reduces the likelihood of inadvertently backing into something.

- A switch on the door of a microwave oven prevents an individual from activating the oven while his or her hand is in it.

- Sensors built into a vehicle's brake pads either give off a sound or trigger a light on the dash when they need to be replaced.

Benchmarking

Rather than trying to come up with its own original ideas, an organization can see what others have done. Benchmarking might involve directly contacting companies that have dealt with similar problems, attending conferences where such issues may be discussed, reading journals/magazines, searching the

Internet, and so forth. Ideally, the organizations selected for study would be those known to be leaders in performance of the relevant process.

TRIZ/ARIZ

Both TRIZ and ARIZ are Russian-developed methodologies that are typically titled *inventive problem solving*. They consist of means for classifying problem characteristics and solutions into dozens of bite-sized ways of looking at them and dealing with them, providing what Wikipedia calls an algorithmic approach to solution generation. In a classic book on the cognitive aspects of designing systems, Donald Norman (1988) includes simpler recommendations such as making errors more difficult or obvious, making it possible to reverse them, and designing the system such that errors do not cause the system to fail.

Cautions on Solution Types

The U.S. Department of Veterans Affairs has an excellent list that organizations should read when identifying potential problem solutions. It classifies various solutions into one of three groups—stronger, intermediate, or weaker. Following is a summary of the types of actions falling into each group:

- Stronger—Physical changes to the environment or process; standardize or simplify the process

- Intermediate—Job aids; reduce similar items/language and distractions

- Weaker—Training, warnings (oral or written); adding another check

A comment on training is worthwhile. If all that is done is to put things back the way they used to be, such as replacing an incorrect document, training will have no effect. Perhaps better expressed—if all that is done is to address the physical cause, training is not likely to be needed. If, however, the process is changed to address the system cause, then training is obviously worthwhile and likely necessary.

A problem is that people think that the training itself is the solution, which almost will never be correct unless the cause was that the individuals had not been trained in the first place. If they had been, then retraining them is not likely to make a difference, unless the reason the training didn't work before is found and addressed.

And finally, training is likely to be done in nearly all cases if for no other reason than to show due diligence. If there had been a failure and it were to show up in a courtroom, not being able to show that people were "trained" would likely be interpreted (incorrectly in most cases) as an inadequate response. Regardless of whether the organization calls it training, individuals involved in the process should be made aware of the problem, the cause and the solution, and their role in carrying it out and watching for future occurrences of the problem. However, they must also understand that the training alone is unlikely to be an effective solution.

STEP 7: SELECT SOLUTION(S) TO BE IMPLEMENTED

Once a list of possible solutions has been generated, the solutions must be sorted through to identify the one(s) to be implemented. While this might seem like a simple task, choosing the wrong solution can offset all the work that has been done to find the exact causes of the problem.

Two major issues need to be considered relative to the decision-making process: (1) who should make the decision, and (2) what criteria should be used to make it? There are many tools that can be used to support the decision-making process.

Who Should Decide?

Vroom and Jago (1976) and many others have written on the advantages and disadvantages of various decision-making techniques. It is important to understand that there is no one correct method, but it will instead depend on the particular situation. Following is a simple classification framework for decision approaches:

- *Autonomous*—The individual (or group) makes the decision on the basis of what he or she knows and/or believes to be best.

- *Consultative*—The individual (or group) makes the decision, but only after first getting input from others who may have knowledge about the situation or who will be involved in carrying out the solution.

- *Consensus*—The individual (or group) shares the decision-making process equally with others with knowledge of or responsibility for the change. That is, discussion is carried out until all agree on the best decision.

Issues that impact which approach is best include the following:

- How much knowledge does the individual (or group) have relative to others who might be involved?

- How much time is available for making the decision? That is, how critical is it to take action quickly?

- How much will lack of input impact willingness of others to support the change?

What Criteria Should Be Used?

The specific criteria used will, of course, also have a dramatic impact on potential results. Typical criteria include the following:

- Potential technical gains to be achieved, such as reduction in errors, improvement of throughput, and so forth

- Financial return such as benefit/cost ratio or payback period

- How long it will take

- How well it will fit with the organizational systems and culture

An important consideration not often considered is what other problems the solution(s) might create. Solving one problem by creating another isn't a particularly efficient way of managing processes, and it will certainly frustrate people. Identification of potential problems should consider both the people/processes directly affected by the solution and the ripple effects those changes may have on other related processes.

Tools to Assist the Decision-Making Process

As with other aspects of problem solving, there are techniques that can aid the analysis of possible solutions. Four relatively well-known techniques follow.

Payoff Matrix

Used by GE's workout process, the *payoff matrix* is a simple 2×2 matrix with *effort* on the x axis and *payoff* on the y axis (Ulrich, Kerr, and Ashkenas 2002). If a solution requires minimum effort and is expected to yield a good payoff, it's considered a no-brainer—do it! If it will yield a small payoff, it will likely be done just because it doesn't require much effort. However, if a solution requires a lot of effort with minimum payoff, it's not likely to be attempted.

Decision Table

A more detailed approach is a *decision table* (see Table 8.2). It allows decision makers to specify the criteria used and to score each possible solution, with the one getting the highest

Table 8.2 Decision table.

Solution option	Evaluation criteria				
	Benefits vs. costs	Timing	Personnel resistance	Technical effectiveness	Total
Purchase new fixtures	9	9	9	9	(36)
Rework current fixtures	3	3	1	3	10
Wait till next design cycle	1	1	1	9	12

score being the most viable. Modifications may be made to the standard table:

- Use a nonlinear scale for scoring, as was done in Table 8.2 (1 = low, 3 = medium, 9 = high), which helps reduce the probability that most solutions will total a similar amount, which often happens if a linear 1–5 or 1–10 scale is used.

- Weight various criteria relative to their importance by multiplying the scores of that specific criterion by a relative weighting number.

Paired Comparison

The *paired comparison* approach requires considering only two solutions at a time (see Table 8.3). Each combination of two solutions is evaluated by each person, who selects one of the two (note that for the A/B combination in the table, 8 of the 10 people voting chose A over B). The same is done for each pair, and the total points for each solution (A, B, C, and D) are computed.

Table 8.3 Paired comparison.

	A/B	A/C	A/D	B/C	B/D	C/D	Total
A	[8]	[7]	[6]				㉑
B	[2]			[6]	[5]		13
C		[3]		[4]		[4]	11
D			[4]		[5]	[6]	15
Total	10	10	10	10	10	10	60

DeBono's Six Thinking Hats

Rather than focusing specifically on decision criteria, the methodology of six thinking hats focuses on ensuring that a good range of thinking perspectives is used by a group to evaluate an idea. They include the following (DeBono):

- Blue Hat—This perspective focuses on making sure the thinking process is managed.

- Green Hat—This thinking mode is intended to expand the list of current ideas.

- Yellow Hat—This is the optimistic view—what are we hoping for?

- White Hat—This mode of thinking is where what is known or what is needed to be known is discussed.

- Red Hat—During this time period, participants express their gut feelings about the solution.

- Black Hat—This is the time to look at the potential downsides.

Other Issues for Solution Selection

A solution may need to be selected for multiple causes, whether physical and/or system. Additionally, solutions should be implemented for both the cause(s) that created the problem and the failures of any barriers.

Unless the known relationship between cause and solution is absolute, consideration should also be given to testing solutions prior to implementation. Testing might include a pilot study, a controlled experiment, or computer modeling. Monte Carlo simulation might also be desired in order to more fully evaluate the range of possible outcomes.

A final recommendation is to consider what is known as Occam's razor, which states that the simplest solution is often the best. There is a tendency of some people to prefer complex, unique, and/or elaborate solutions, but usually these are not only more costly and more difficult to implement, but also less predictable.

9

Implement, Evaluate, and Institutionalize

STEP 8: IMPLEMENT THE SOLUTION(S)

Finding a good solution is one thing, but effectively implementing it is another. With the former it's all cognitive, but with the latter it's all about getting organizational resources very focused for a specific period of time. Implementation calls for management of three knowledge areas:

- *Technology*—This is having a proper understanding of the technology in the process that will be changed. Depending on the organization and the problem, it could include chemistry, computer science, law, metals machining, medicine, and so forth. Technical decisions based on the technology must be made, and any information or equipment required for implementation must be acquired if it does not already exist in the organization. Since this aspect of implementation planning is highly dependent on each organization's technology, it cannot be dealt with in this book.

- *Project management*—This is the generic process for creating the schedule for implementation, acquiring and organizing the resources, and communicating and carrying out the action plan. There are many fine references for project management, so it will not be dealt with here in any detail, but a few relevant pointers will be provided.

- *Organizational change management*—This involves recognizing that any change will meet some level of resistance and thus taking action to reduce or mediate it so the change will be more successful and less stressful. Experience indicates that most organizations ignore this issue at their peril (and they wonder why things don't go well!). The topic will be covered in Chapter 10.

Project Management Pointers

Project management is about getting things done at the right time using the resources allocated to the project. However, the right time can be affected by whether the estimates are based on forward or backward scheduling. With forward scheduling one predicts how long each activity/phase of the project will take and then schedules out to determine when the project will be completed. Backward scheduling sets a date by which the project is to be completed and then sets schedules and allocates resources for each activity in order to accomplish it.

Regardless of the scheduling method used, the implementation plan needs to be documented, communicated, and tracked in order to maintain the change. An action plan tracking form (see Table 9.1) is often used to track the day-to-day activities. A key to keeping the project on track is to never remove a missed date from the "When" column, as it causes useful information to disappear that can highlight problem areas. Instead, the missed date should be marked through and the revised date added below it.

Some specific issues that should be included in the project plan (if appropriate) are the following:

- Development and execution of a validation protocol to ensure that the process change is robust

Table 9.1 Action plan tracking form.

Item	Action	Responsible	When	Status
1				
2				
3				
4				
5				
6				
7				
8				

- Revisions to and approval of procedures and other relevant information sources to get them in line with the change

- How the change will be communicated to those responsible for carrying it out, and any training necessary

- How effectiveness of the change will be evaluated

- Contingency plan for what to do if the change goes awry

The organization should also be aware of the need to separate the process of planning for implementation from the process of actually carrying out the plan. Not only will they be done at different times, but in some cases by different people. Effective communication is obviously critical.

STEP 9: EVALUATE THE EFFECT(S)

There's a reason the Check/Study step is in the PDCA/PDSA model, and it's because the most significant learning often occurs when things turn out differently than was expected. Taking action without checking to see whether the process improvement worked is like shooting in the dark.

Follow-up should first look at the *Y* variable to see whether performance of the process is back to what is normal or expected, but the *X* variable should also be checked to ensure that the change has been properly implemented. Following is the rationale:

Figure 9.1 shows that there are not two but four possible combinations of Y and X. If we find that Y improved, we assume that X is responsible, and if Y didn't improve it is because X wasn't effectively implemented. However, there are two other possibilities:

- *Y might get better even though X wasn't effectively implemented. This sometimes occurs because people know that attention is being paid to performance, known as the Hawthorne effect (Okes and Westcott 2001). The solution therefore needs to be implemented more effectively (redo Step 8) and the results reevaluated.*

- *The other possibility is that although X was effectively implemented, Y did not improve. This indicates the possibility that the solution may not be the right one, or that the correct cause was not found, or that the cause-and-effect relationships within the system are not well understood. In this case Steps 1–7 may need to be revised.*

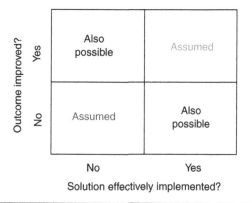

Figure 9.1   Solution-outcome matrix.

STEP 10: INSTITUTIONALIZE THE CHANGE

It's always nice to get to this point in the corrective action or problem-solving process. After all, the process is now performing as it should, perhaps even better than ever before. However, keeping it that way is another story!

The first thing to be done, if it wasn't fully completed prior to implementation, is standardization. This means updating any relevant documents, databases, software, and so forth, that weren't revised prior to implementation. For example, do job descriptions need to be changed on the basis of what was learned? Does the content of training materials need to be improved? How about FMEAs, control plans, and so forth?

The next step is to spread what was learned to other areas/processes/facilities where the same or similar problem has the potential to occur, or where the solution would improve performance. This is a component of the knowledge management process that every organization should have. The knowledge transfer process may be relatively informal, such as a lessons-learned database, or more structured through formal meetings designed to cross-deploy ideas.

The final component of institutionalization is to sustain the gain over the long term. This often involves formal tracking of Y for some longer period of time, and auditing the process (the X variable) to ensure that the desired process controls are being properly maintained. The idea is to sustain the new process until it becomes accepted and integrated into how the organization does business. Some additional ways for doing this include the following:

- Make it impossible to do it the old way (for example, remove equipment, information, and so forth, required by the previous process)

- Include adoption of change as a component of personnel evaluations

- Revise the reward system to include consideration of flexibility

- Have personnel who work in the changed process assess the degree of success and then report on the successes, difficulties, and perceived barriers

- Have downstream customers affected by the change provide regular feedback on their perceptions of success

- Hold the process owner responsible for maintaining the change

- Shape organizational culture and norms to support the changes

Until the change is fully internalized by the individuals responsible for its implementation, there is a risk of reverting back to the old way. However, since these individuals work within an organizational system, not only individual but also group and organizational structures need to be involved in realignment and reinforcement of change.

10

Organizational Issues

Because root cause analysis is a logical, rational technical process, it should come as no surprise to anyone who has been in the workplace for some time to hear that there are also human issues that can significantly impact the ability of an organization to effectively find and address problem causes. This chapter reviews some of the most common issues, which can apply to individuals, groups, and/or the entire organization.

COGNITIVE BIASES

While humans may believe that their thinking is rational and accurate according to the information available, there is much evidence that emotions often cause them to interpret information in ways that suit their particular needs. Following are some of the many possible biases along with examples of the potential effects on problem-solving effectiveness and/or efficiency.

Anchoring Bias

Anchoring occurs when recent data are compared with previous data, and if the recent data are better, they are assumed to be good. Advertisers do this all the time when they give a "regular" price and a "sale" price, which causes people to believe they're getting a bargain. However, the sale price may actually be entirely out of alignment relative to the value or competitive pricing from other sources. An example in problem solving might be interpreting that since the Y variable got better, the process is working fine, when in fact it might still be producing results that are unacceptable to some stakeholders.

Recency Effect

With the *recency effect*, people remember the most recent occurrence better than similar or conflicting information heard earlier. People who purport to give both sides of the story may use this to present the alternative view first, then their own, preferred view, which is more likely to be remembered since it is the last thing the listener hears. In root cause analysis, people might assume that if a problem recurs, it is due to the same reason as the previous time. This might cause them to ignore other possible causes and perhaps to waste a lot of time looking in the wrong area.

Confirmation Bias

People want to be correct in their beliefs; thus they tend to look for data that confirm them. For example, after purchasing a new car an individual often feels validated when noticing that others are driving the same model. In root cause analysis the tendency may be to look for data only to confirm one's causal theory, while good analytical thinking also requires looking for data that might disconfirm it, especially before spending considerable time and money to implement a solution.

Availability Bias

Herbert Simon, an expert on decision making, believed that humans, rather than trying to truly optimize their decisions, tend to be somewhat lazy and instead satisfice, investing the minimum effort to achieve an acceptable decision (Plous 1993). In root cause analysis this might play out as collecting only data that are easy to get rather than what would be more definitive.

Recall Bias

Perhaps recall bias should be called recall error, as this bias is based on how easily the thought process can go down the wrong path when an individual is trying to remember something. Rather than recalling what is actually true, an individual recalls something similar or something that is less/more dramatic. This is an obvious source of error when using interviews to collect data, as the interviewee may be unable to differentiate between what is accurate and what is imagined.

Overuse of Heuristics

Experience is obviously a good thing, as it allows one to learn the different nuances involved in a particular subject. It lets people develop mental algorithms that allow them to make rapid and accurate decisions. However, this experience and speed can also cause problem solvers to ignore evidence that is to the contrary, or to dive in too deeply without taking a broader view of the problem.

Making Assumptions

It's probably valid to assume that it will take approximately 24 hours for the earth to rotate and that the sun will therefore rise each day. However, during problem diagnosis, assumptions are often made about what actions occurred, how a particular piece of equipment works, or the content of an information source. This isn't to say that assumptions shouldn't be made, but when they are and an error could result, they should be made explicit so they can be verified if things aren't progressing as expected.

RESISTANCE TO CHANGE

As has been mentioned a couple of places in the book, when something is about to be changed, there will be some people who don't like the idea. It doesn't really matter whether the reasons are rational, as either way the change will produce resistance, overt or covert, that must be overcome.

A summary of some of the key reasons people resist change is presented in Figure 10.1. It basically comes down to the following: (1) people are familiar and often comfortable with the way things are now, (2) they fear change they believe might negatively impact them, and (3) the process of change is poorly managed by the organization.

Many authors have written about ways to understand the sources of this resistance and how to alleviate them. Stephen Covey (1989) uses circles of influence to point out how our time and attention are often misplaced. Figure 10.2 shows a similar

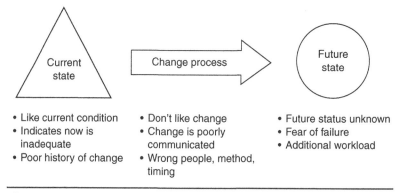

• Like current condition	• Don't like change	• Future status unknown
• Indicates now is inadequate	• Change is poorly communicated	• Fear of failure
• Poor history of change	• Wrong people, method, timing	• Additional workload

Figure 10.1 Reasons people resist change.

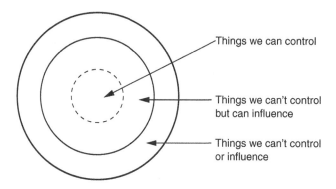

Figure 10.2 Clarifying what we can/can't affect.

concept that can help people understand that some things are totally outside their control, so there is no reason to worry about them. Other things are perhaps out of their control but individuals may be able to influence them, and still others are totally in their control. Helping people differentiate among these can help them feel less powerless and better focus their mental energy.

Everett Rogers (1995) used a normal distribution to describe the rate at which individuals adopt a new technology, which can be generalized as flexibility to change. He classified people into one of five groups, going from earliest to latest adopters: (1) innovators, (2) early adopters, (3) early majority, (4) late majority, and (5) laggards. In an organization, one might presume there is a similar distribution of how people will respond to a new idea. When implementing a change it is certainly useful to involve some of the leading-edge folks, who are always ready to try something new. However, it is the core/majority that will cause the change to succeed or fail, so this group also needs to be represented. One should be cautious about leaving the laggards totally out, because if they're not at all involved, they may try to sabotage the effort.

Force field analysis (Figure 10.3) is one way to bring together and analyze some of the issues specific to a particular change initiative. The idea is to write down the reasons why people will support the change (called "motivators" in the figure) as well as the reasons why they will resist it (the "fears").

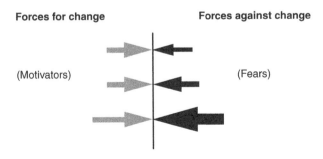

Forces for change **Forces against change**

(Motivators) (Fears)

Figure 10.3 Force field analysis.

By being clear about the reasons and relative strengths of each (represented by the size of the arrow in the figure), plans can be made to leverage the motivators and reduce or offset the fears.

So resistance will be met, but in many cases it can be predicted, planned for, and mitigated. The choice of how to deal with it is also wide ranging, as demonstrated by Figure 10.4, which the author developed on the basis of complexity theory. It indicates that an organization/group/individual can be shaped by providing high-level input such as clarifying the values of the organization and/or creating/modifying policies effectively aligned to the desired behaviors. This is a push orientation, but a pull orientation can also be applied by asking for and shaping the desired outputs through setting and communicating proper goals aligned to desires, and providing rewards when the behaviors and goals are forthcoming.

In the middle are different types of levers dealing with the day-to-day operation of the organization. One is to simply change the individual; that is, get rid of him or her if he or she is creating chaos, or move this person to another role if he or she is not capable of performing in the current one. Another is to leverage the power of groups by creating connections among people. Cross-functional teams are one form of connections, as are electronic means used to allow people to virtually work together regardless of their geographic location.

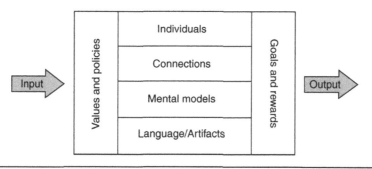

Figure 10.4 Changing a complex adaptive system.

Changing mental models involves helping people gain a new understanding of themselves or how the organization operates. Education and training are two means of doing so, and job rotation for the purpose of development is another. Finally, there are the less apparent factors such as the language used in the organization as well as the physical environment in which people work. Changing these can provide subtle but powerful nudges toward new behaviors.

ORGANIZATIONAL CULTURE

The culture of an organization consists of the often unstated, but which often appear to be hardwired, habits that shape how people behave. How an organization perceives root cause analysis, problem solving, and corrective action can have a dramatic impact on how effective the outcomes are likely to be. Figure 10.5 demonstrates how a culture where problems are seen as reasons for reprisal will result in a self-fulfilling tendency toward poor investigations and therefore poor solutions, resulting in a repeat of the problem.

Instead, organizations should learn from Dr. W. Edwards Deming's modification of the PDCA cycle to PDSA, emphasizing that improvement is about learning. The reason problems occur is often because something is misunderstood somewhere in the organization, and how the process is operated

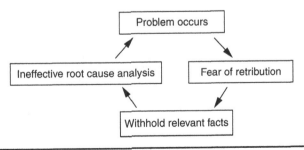

Figure 10.5 Impact of a punitive culture on root cause analysis.

turns out to create problems somewhere downstream. Viewing the problem-solving process as a learning process can make it a fun process!

PROJECT OWNERSHIP

A final issue, which some organizations are beginning to recognize, is who should be responsible for conducting the root cause analysis? All too often it's QA personnel who do the diagnosis and then recommend a solution to the individual responsible for the process that failed. This has the advantage of using the skills that QA personnel are often more likely to have, but it is a major disadvantage in that the owner of the process to be changed has little knowledge of the rationale behind the conclusions.

Instead, why not have the process owner take responsibility for the corrective action, with QA personnel providing coaching as needed? In other words, QA personnel facilitate the process (discussed in the next section) but do not take responsibility for decisions outside their scope of control. There are times when this may not be feasible, such as when the problem boundaries are initially so broad that it would be difficult to know who owns the problem. In this case some initial investigation may be needed in order to more narrowly define the scope. Also, in highly regulated industries and/or in potential high-risk problem situations, it may be necessary for a highly trained root cause analyst to lead the investigation. Such is often the case for investigations of major accidents.

COACHING/FACILITATION SKILLS

If someone is called upon to coach or facilitate the root cause analysis process, it is useful to know what this means. Following is an overview of facilitation (coaching is simply a slightly more active role), including the different roles one can take, what might need to be facilitated, and ways to do so.

Content versus Process Knowledge

When an organization, group, or individual needs help there are different roles from which they can choose. They could look for someone with content expertise in the area where they need help, such as in chemistry, computers, transportation routes, and so forth. Or if they believe they have sufficient content knowledge but are having difficulty making sense of it in a particular context, they may look for someone who can help them process that knowledge.

Figure 10.6 shows five types of helpers they might look for, depending on which form of help they most desire. For example, an IT group trying to solve a computer software problem might bring in as an external consultant one of the following five types:

- *Expert*: The consultant would be someone who is a computer software expert and who would perform the diagnosis and likely also recommend (and perhaps implement) a solution to the problem.

- *Trainer*: The consultant would provide the IT group with training in software problems, troubleshooting techniques, and types of solutions that could be applied. The group would then carry out its own diagnosis.

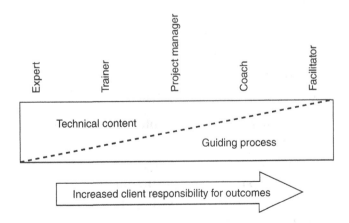

Figure 10.6 Types of helpers.

- *Project manager*: The consultant would work as lead person with a team of individuals from the IT group to guide the diagnosis and problem resolution.

- *Coach*: The consultant would ask questions about what the group has done so far to try to diagnose the problem. He or she would help the group understand where it may have gone wrong as well as provide additional options.

- *Facilitator*: The consultant would sit in on meetings where the group was discussing the problem and trying to perform the diagnosis. When the consultant believed some input would be useful to help the group go in a more productive direction, she or he would contribute.

While five roles are defined in the figure, it is, of course, actually a continuum, where the consultant provides high IT knowledge and little process knowledge on the expert end, and little IT knowledge and a lot of problem-solving process knowledge on the facilitator end. Someone who works as a facilitator may actually move back and forth across the continuum over the life of his or her relationship with the individual or group, depending on whether he or she has content expertise in the relevant technology and what the scope of the agreement with the client includes.

Types of Facilitators

Let's now assume that a group needing help has the technical (content) expertise but needs support in diagnosing a problem and thus has asked for a root cause facilitator to help them. There are a few different roles the facilitator can take on (see Figure 10.7):

- *Observer facilitator*: In this role the facilitator sits quietly listening to and observing the group. He or she intervenes only when useful or necessary, such as providing advice on which step of the analysis might need to be done next or what tool to use. He or she might also do some coaching with the group leader prior to or after the meeting.

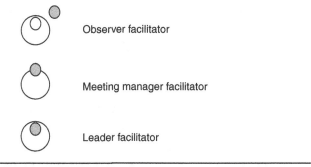

Figure 10.7 Facilitator roles.

- *Meeting manager facilitator*: In this case the facilitator has been asked to lead the meeting, even though she or he has no responsibility for outcomes of the project. The facilitator must be careful not to get involved in discussion of the technology of the project, but should instead concentrate on keeping the group focused on good diagnosis and/or solution generation.

- *Leader facilitator*: In this case the leader of the team has not only content knowledge but also process skills. This is the ideal—where the owner of the process would have good root cause analysis process knowledge. However, he or she may still choose to bring in an observer facilitator at certain stages of the analysis.

Processes to Facilitate

Facilitators can support one or more of three major areas: (1) technical process used by the group to accomplish its mission, (2) effective meeting management, and (3) group dynamics. It is not the intent of this book to cover meeting management or group dynamics, but these are important skills for facilitators.

Technical process facilitation means guiding the individual or group through a series of steps to accomplish a goal. If it were a strategic planning session, then the steps for developing a strategic plan would be applicable. If it were a benchmarking study, the steps for planning and conducting a benchmarking project would be relevant. However, given that the focus of this book is root cause analysis, then the 10-step model, or some alternative the organization or facilitator may have adopted, would be appropriate.

Facilitating the root cause analysis process then involves being aware of where the individual/group is in the diagnostic steps, and how effectively each step is being carried out. The facilitator may choose various means of providing needed advice:

- *Redirect*: Simply state what different approach might be useful based on the difficulties the individual/group is having in the diagnosis.

- *Observe*: Provide feedback on where the individual/group may be struggling and give options for alternative actions.

- *Explore*: Inquire as to how well the individual/group is doing, and what changes, if any, would be useful.

Which of these three approaches is most appropriate will depend on how knowledgeable and experienced the individual/group is, as well as how open they are to external help. It is wise to get agreement with them at the outset as to their expectations.

Many of the same concepts for facilitating a group also apply to a one-on-one coaching process. The coach must have some structured method for evaluating progress and providing feedback. How feedback is delivered will depend on the level of confidence and willingness of the person being coached, as well as the degree of change needed.

Someone coaching/facilitating root cause analysis would ideally be highly experienced in the field. However, another factor that can impact effectiveness is the individual's degree of self-knowledge. For example, if the individual is someone who likes to be in control, he or she may tend to micromanage the process, rather than see it more holistically and as a learning process for all involved. It can be highly useful for anyone taking on the role of facilitator (for any type of work) to know his or her strengths and weaknesses. Assessment instruments such as the DiSC profile, Myer-Briggs, and many others can aid in developing such self-knowledge.

OTHER ISSUES

Where to Do the Work

Although it may appear to be a minor issue, something to consider is where root cause analysis work should be carried out. Should it take place in a conference room or should it take place on the shop floor, in the warehouse, or in the office where the problem occurred or was found? It turns out that both locations are useful (MacDuffie 1997), since each has advantages and impacts.

When developing the problem statement, creating a flow-chart, developing a logic tree of possible causes, or analyzing data, the quiet of a conference room is likely quite useful. However, to broaden understanding, there's nothing like going to where the process is actually carried out, in order to observe and discuss the problem or process with those carrying out the work on a day-to-day basis.

The Time Required

Over and over, people want to know how to do root cause analysis more quickly. Certainly being better at it will probably speed it up some, but the more important issue is that it needs to be done in a way that will actually find and address the causes, thereby greatly reducing the probability of recurrence. So if there is a tradeoff to be made between speed and quality, spending more time would seem to be the better option.

Certainly many audit nonconformities can often be diagnosed and corrected very quickly, but for complex problems it is not unusual for weeks or months to be required. Much of this extended time is likely necessary in order to get the required data, as well as acquiring and installing equipment or other process changes necessary to address the cause.

How to Present Findings

It is not unusual for someone who is a good problem solver to be asked to diagnose a problem for which he or she has no direct responsibility. Presenting the findings to the process owner or others who work in or maintain the failed process can then be a difficult situation. In such a situation it is important to present not only one's conclusions but also at least a portion of the process used to come to those conclusions. This has two advantages: (1) it helps listeners understand that the conclusions are not arbitrary but were instead reached through a logical, objective process, and (2) listeners will learn something about the steps for conducting an effective diagnosis, which they may then be willing to use on their own in the future.

This lesson is especially important when an organization uncovers a problem within its walls that is believed to be due to an external supplier. Simply asking the supplier to take corrective action is likely to be met with some resistance (although it may not be expressed). If instead the organization presents the problem and the steps and data involved that led to the conclusion that it was not an internal problem but instead due to the supplier, the supplier will be much more likely to dedicate resources to performing an investigation.

Another important issue regarding presenting findings is to not overuse the technical language of the root cause tools. Although the individuals to whom the information pertains may be familiar with the concepts, they are less likely to know the specific terminology of the tools (such as Pareto diagram, run chart, or logic tree), which will then detract from their focus. Using more generic terminology (such as "barchart ordered by importance," "looking at the data over time," and "cause-and-effect relationships") may then allow them to pay more attention to the diagnostic approach and conclusions being presented.

11

Human Error and Incident Analysis

As stated in the preface, this book is not intended for readers whose primary interest is in accident investigations or who must deal extensively with human causes of error. However, a book on root cause analysis would not be replete without at least some introductory information on these topics. This chapter summarizes some of the core issues around human error and briefly describes how accident investigations are similar to, but also different from, the types of projects for which this book is primarily intended.

HUMAN ERROR

Human error is obviously always going to exist. Both research and experience indicate that in many cases it is actually caused or abetted by system design errors. Yes, these design errors are also probably errors created by humans, but if the process for designing systems were more mistake-proof . . . you get the picture.

There are two major components involved in human error: the human and the environment (system) in which she or he works. Human errors can be broken down into categories of physical versus cognitive errors. Figure 11.1 demonstrates this concept using an input-process-output model whereby the

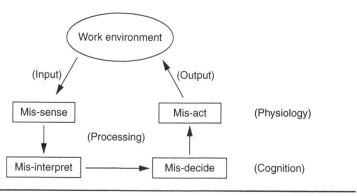

Figure 11.1   Macro causes of human error.

human takes in information from the environment through the five senses, processes this information, and then acts based on the decision made.

A car accident has occurred because a driver pulled out into traffic at the wrong time and was rear-ended. This could be caused by the following:

• *Not seeing the oncoming car due to eyesight problems (mis-sense)*

• *Seeing the car but misinterpreting the speed at which it was moving*

• *Seeing the car and correctly interpreting the speed, but deciding to try to beat it (but the laws of physics won out)*

• *Seeing the car, correctly interpreting the speed, correctly deciding there was enough time to pull out, but when doing so the driver's foot slipped off the accelerator (mis-act), causing the car to abruptly slow down*

Of course, the car accident could also have been a function of the environment, such as a curve just preceding the side road where the driver was pulling out, with too high a speed limit for cars to be able to safely pull out. The point is that when something goes wrong, even though it may involve a human situation and be truly a human error, the cause of that error should be explored at a depth sufficient to allow effective corrective action.

Environmental Causes

Human errors caused by the environment can be of many types. Following are typical categories and some examples:

- Poor design of the interface between equipment and people: Imagine a computer screen that is placed at an incorrect angle, causing a glare that makes reading text nearly impossible.

- Improper work pace: Most people know that if a process requires working too fast, errors are more likely, but the same is often true if the pace is too slow, causing boredom and lack of attention.

- Destructive work schedule: There's a reason that airline pilots are required to have eight hours of rest and that truck drivers are limited in the number of hours they work. The human body needs adequate rest to perform well.

- Unclear presentation of information: This can be simple things such as font type and size, or more complex issues such as language or terminology used (written or spoken).

- Disruptive environmental factors: Noise, lighting, or temperature can create problems by negatively affecting physical or cognitive functioning.

- Poor ergonomic design: If processes are designed in such a way that they require abnormal or uncomfortable seating, reach, walking, and so forth, errors are more likely to result.

- Problems with resources/equipment: Equipment failure might not allow an individual to properly complete a task that has already been started.

- Interruption of work routine: An individual can lose track of where she or he was in a sequence of activities when something or someone creates a distraction.

- Inattentive culture: Some organizations do not attempt to build a culture where attention to detail (whether related to quality, safety, and so forth) is understood as the norm and critical to keeping the organization functioning at a high level of performance.

Human Causes

There are also aspects of human beings that can lead to errors, including the following:

- Physical size: An individual's height, reach, and so forth, can impact his or her ability to carry out certain activities.

- Physical senses: An individual uses the five senses (sight, smell, hearing, touch, and taste) to gain information to be processed. If these signals are incorrect, further processing is unlikely to be improved.

- Motor skills: The result of a human decision is some action, whether in the form of speaking, moving, or otherwise interacting with the environment. Things such as coordination, flexibility, and dexterity can therefore affect how well someone performs a particular activity.

- Cognitive capacity and skills: In the information age this will increasingly be important, as it has been for many years for the proverbial rocket scientists, brain surgeons, and their equivalents in other sectors.

- Qualifications: Although an individual may have the basic functional abilities, if his or her experience or training is not sufficient for a particular activity, mistakes will be more likely due to a lack of knowledge.

- Health/physiology: An individual who is sick, hungry, or otherwise affected by physiological problems can have lowered physical and/or mental functioning, resulting in a decreased capacity to perform well.

- Psychological state: Someone under significant emotional distress could be limited in his or her ability to carry out some activities.

Human error guru James Reason (1990) defined two types of human error, slips and lapses, which could be the result of these human or environmental factors. These categories should perhaps be reserved for times when none of the factors listed can be specifically identified as the cause, recognizing that sometimes things happen that simply cannot be explained.

Solutions for Human Errors

The solutions for addressing human error typically fall into one or more of the following categories:

- Matching people to the job: This involves making sure that the individual's physical, cognitive, and emotional capacities are sufficient for the requirements demanded by the job. The capabilities might be determined through reviews of previous performance or through extensive testing.

- Education and/or training: While an individual may have the basic capacities required, he or she may still need additional knowledge in order to perform more effectively.

- Standardize the process: Chaos is almost always going to produce more unwanted variation than a standardized process. The latter reduces the cognitive load for people who must carry it out.

- Clearer instructions, samples, or other job aids: Standardization may be good, but if it is contained in detailed instructions no one can or will read, it's useless. For many activities it is better to provide examples of what is and is not acceptable, along with flowcharts, diagrams, or photos that demonstrate what is to be done.

- Mistake-proofing: As discussed in Chapter 8, designing the process to where it is impossible to do things incorrectly is obviously the optimum approach, if it can be done cost effectively.

- Changes to the environment/system/process: While some of the earlier solutions can also fit into this category, it specifically recognizes that sometimes a process is simply too complex or fault-prone. Identifying and resolving the characteristics of the product or process design that make it so is what root cause analysis and problem solving are all about.

Is It Really an Error?

Although a human may indeed appear to be the cause of the problem, there are three questions that are helpful for identifying what the underlying issue may be. They should be asked in the following sequence:

1. *Does the individual know how to perform the activity?* Just because the individual has been trained does not mean he or she knows how. The training itself may have been ineffective, or evaluation of the individual's knowledge may have been incorrect. However, if the individual knows how to perform the activity, the next question should be asked.

2. *Is the individual capable?* Although the individual may have been through what is known to be an effective training program, there may be physical limitations that prevent him or her from reliably carrying out the activity. If, however, the individual both knows and is capable, then the next question should be asked.

3. *Is the individual willing?* Sometimes it's neither a knowledge nor a capability issue, but instead a motivational issue. The individual may simply not want to do the job properly, due to poor self-motivation or poor people management.

INCIDENT ANALYSIS

For accident investigations the same five diagnostic steps are used but are typically done in a different order. Some reasons for the difference are that there is no standard process for having an accident (although there may be a process that should have been followed but wasn't), and more importantly, that the data need to be gathered quickly. For example, interviews conducted of people involved will be much less useful or accurate if conducted a couple of weeks later, rather than almost immediately.

Following is a reordering of the five diagnostic steps of the 10-step model for incident investigation applications:

1. Define the problem

2. Collect the data

3. Analyze the data

4. Understand the process

5. Identify possible causes

So the process still begins with problem definition, but there is likely not as much detail as would be typical for a repetitive problem. The next step is to immediately gather as much data as possible. Examples of data collection include the following:

- Getting photographs of the accident site as well as video recordings that may have been used to monitor security

- Locating, labeling, and controlling any failed devices needing to be analyzed

- Interviewing people directly involved with the accident as well as those located near the accident site

- Getting documents used to initiate the work where the accident occurred

- Finding records that allow seeing what occurred and when, such as manual or computerized logs

Analyzing the data involves putting the information into a time-order sequence. This leads to being able to then flowchart the series of activities/events that occurred (see Figure 11.2).

Once the flowchart is developed it can be analyzed for what occurred that shouldn't have or what should have happened that didn't. Causes (often called causal factors [Rooney and Vanden Heuvel 2004]) are then flagged for further analysis. This analysis may then lead to the use of a logic tree to drill down deeper to find underlying causes. These diagnoses are also iterative in that as data are analyzed and the process and possible causes are identified, it is likely that more data may be searched out in order to understand what happened in more detail.

Since incidents are typically higher-impact problems, not only will causal factors be determined and acted on but so will contributing factors. As mentioned earlier, contributing factors are those issues that could not, by themselves, have caused the problem to occur. However, addressing them will often significantly reduce the probability of recurrence, since either they were a factor that helped create the problem or they did not detect the problem earlier.

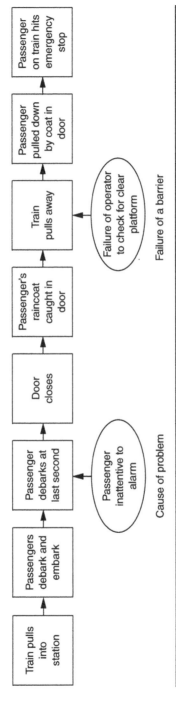

Figure 11.2 Flowchart of an incident.

12

Improving Corrective Action

Both preventive and corrective action are about managing risk. Preventive action is a proactive means for assessing processes for potential risk and putting in controls to reduce the probability and/or the impact. Performance of those processes is then monitored through both metrics (the Y) and audits (the X). When problems are found, a decision is made as to whether corrective action is warranted; if it is, root cause analysis is used to identify and resolve weaknesses in the process, thereby installing additional controls. The two processes then create a continuous loop (see Figure 12.1).

Diagnosing a problem consists of three major components: (1) the problem statement, (2) theories about possible causes, and (3) evidence to support or refute each cause (see Figure 12.2). However, if only these three steps were provided as a diagnostic guide, people would likely jump directly to possible causes without thinking about the process or spend insufficient time thinking about what data need to be collected before doing so. In other words, getting people to slow down, not speed up, is necessary in order to perform an effective diagnosis.

Getting people to slow down isn't easy when their emotions take control. Arbitrarily set time requirements for responding

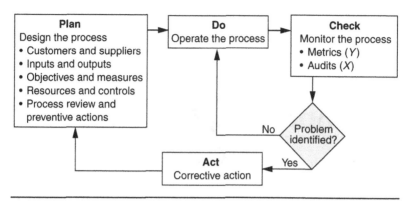

Figure 12.1 Preventive and corrective action.

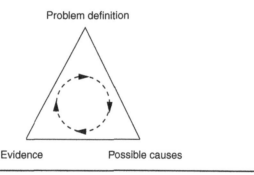

Figure 12.2 Major components for problem diagnosis.

to corrective action requests, an organizational culture that sees corrective action requests as hot potatoes, and the sense that people have too much on their plate are just some of the causes of such emotions.

What is needed is a way to get the neocortex (the logical, objective portion of the brain) to take control, rather than the reptilian portion that causes automatic fight-or-flight responses. Although it may be difficult to get organizations to adopt the following studies, the author has found them to be quite useful for helping keep one's sanity in potentially emotional situations.

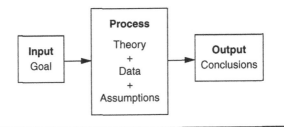

Figure 12.3 Thinking as a process.

CRITICAL THINKING

Many people go through life with little-to-no reflective thinking. Critical thinking is taking time to think about one's own thinking processes, how effective they are, and how they might be improved. Figure 12.3 is one view of the components of critical thinking, which can be equally applied to thinking about how one approaches a problem.

The goal drives what theories are used to analyze the situation, what data will be acquired, and what assumptions are made. Conclusions made are a result of how well all these are properly understood and processed by all involved. While the 10-step model attempts to help with the goal (through Step 1), the theory (through Steps 2 and 3), and the data (Steps 4 and 5), it does not specifically address assumptions. A rule of thumb is that problem solvers should explicitly state their assumptions, especially when they have reached some sort of impasse.

BUDDHISM

A major component of the Buddhist philosophy is about stilling one's mind, rather than allowing distractions such as attachment to things, people, or ideas to cloud one's thinking and decisions. While the Eightfold Path is designed to help one live a more enlightened life, certain components could equally well be applied to organizational problem solving, such as the following:

- *Right view*: Seeing things as they really are rather than how we'd like them to be, which will allow a more realistic understanding of what one is dealing with.

- *Right thought and right speech*: Not criticizing those who created the problem or who have not been successful in solving it.

- *Right effort, right mindfulness, and right contemplation*: Staying focused on the problem rather than wandering off on side issues.

STOIC PHILOSOPHY

In short, what is, is. Or put another way, stuff happens, but one can choose whether to allow it to create stress and the resulting negative impacts on emotional and physical health, or accept what is and move forward. In a study of individuals who had survived catastrophes of various kinds, it was found that those who accepted the reality of their situation and looked objectively at what they could do were much more likely to survive (Gonzales 2005).

An individual once said to the author, "There's a bird in my house. What does that mean?" The author responded, "It means there's a bird in your house."

This is a simple example of one of these philosophies applied to an everyday situation. Presence of a bird inside a building causes concerns or curiosity based on superstitions that have been passed along from generation to generation. However, such meanings are placed on the situation by the person, rather than being an inherent, objective part of it. As

Toyota's A3 thinking emphasizes, logical thinking and objectivity are key components required for effective problem solving (Sobek and Smalley 2008).

SUMMARY OF ROOT CAUSE ANALYSIS

Root cause analysis is a process for finding the causes of problems so that solutions can be aligned to those causes. While knowledge of the underlying technology involved in the failed process is necessary, it is not sufficient to provide a rigorous diagnosis. General process improvement can also benefit from many of the techniques presented in this book. However, with process improvement, one is often trying to optimize a working process rather than fix one that has failed.

The model presented can be used to solve problems or to look at repetitive causes, which simply begins at a deeper level of the system. It can also be used for near misses if information on such events is recorded. Success with the model will be affected by how finitely the cause-and-effect relationships are known or can be defined. For example, the natural laws of physics are known and pretty discrete, which makes troubleshooting of equipment failures generally easy.

When software is involved, the situation becomes more complex since the decisions being made are less visible. And when the problem involves human behavior, complexity is even greater, since the fallibility of the human mind plus the impact of differing beliefs and values makes relationships between causes and effects appear invisible. Availability of data can also make analysis difficult, such as in situations where there are no specifications, standards, or history for comparison, or where data are not available (such as when evidence is destroyed as part of the failure) or are difficult to obtain (such as when it is contained within physical or legal boundaries).

It is expected that the model will be useful for beginning, intermediate, and advanced problem solvers in the following ways:

• For beginners, the model can provide a guideline that they can use as they begin learning problem solving.

• For intermediate-level problem solvers, the model can provide an explicit view into what they may currently be doing and help them fine-tune their thinking.

• For advanced personnel, it will likely be most useful for when they think they have solved a problem, only to find it coming back again. This may indicate a need to step back from the heuristics they have been using and look at the problem more broadly.

The author has been involved with many problem-solving projects, many of them having a significant financial impact. The 10-step model is the embodiment of much of what was learned during these projects and through teaching the process to others. Readers are encouraged to try the model and adapt it as needed for their own use. For those who find the diagnostic process especially invigorating, learning about the statistical techniques that can supplement this logical thinking could provide another source of significant leverage for problem solving.

Appendix A

Example Projects

Although throughout the chapters there were many examples of portions of root cause analysis projects, this appendix provides a more complete view of several from different industries and situations. The major focus is on the diagnostic process, Steps 1–5 of the 10-step model.

The examples are intentionally simple ones, but the reader is reminded that the primary differences between simple and complicated diagnoses are the number of possible causes and the levels one must drill down. It may be handy to have a copy of the 10-step model available while reading the descriptions so as to trace the steps of the model through each activity taken in the project.

A NEED FOR FOCUS

Management requested that a team of employees reduce downtime on a production line. It was a continuous process, meaning that if one piece of equipment on the line went down, the entire line had to stop. When it stopped, one portion of the line had to continue to operate, but dump what was being produced into a scrap heap.

Management asked that a root cause facilitator meet with the team members to observe them. The team had primarily been brainstorming causes and solutions for two meetings, and the facilitator, in order to help them get more focused, requested that they develop a process flowchart. (It was so simple that they probably thought he was crazy; see Figure A.1.)

Once the flowchart was done, he asked, "Which machine is down most often?" (Note: Try to avoid working on really broad problems. Reduce line downtime by reducing machine downtime; focusing on the one that is down the most will have the biggest impact.) There was consensus that it was probably Machine A, but the facilitator requested data to support their opinions.

So the team gathered data (it was real-time data collected at the line, not data from maintenance records) and organized it into a Pareto diagram (see Figure A.2). The diagram indicated that Machine B had the most downtime, which was a surprise to the team since Machine A was much more complex and visible when it went down.

The team now had data indicating which machine contributed the most to downtime and how much it was down within

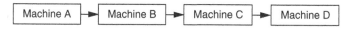

Figure A.1   Process flowchart for continuous line.

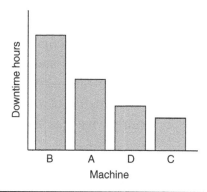

Figure A.2   Line downtime by machine.

a certain period of time. They could now write a problem statement and focus on that specific problem.

The next step was to find out why Machine B was down. So the team returned to data collection, but this time the members not only focused on just how much it was down but also classified the causes of downtime into categories. The next Pareto (see Figure A.3) showed that board changes were the largest cause. (Note: Had the team relied on maintenance records, this cause would not even have shown up, since it was not something that maintenance was involved with. It was an operator-responsible task, similar to replacing a worn tool.)

An investigation into the board change process found that when the machine was new, one person could do the task in about five minutes. In the current state it requires two people and about 20 minutes. This is due to wear of some of the machine component parts (the product being produced is very abrasive).

The team quantified the cost of the downtime and approached management with a recommendation that certain portions of the machine be rebuilt. Downtime of the line was reduced by 6 percentage points as a result of this repair, saving the company hundreds of thousands of dollars of downtime.

The machine wear was obviously only the physical cause. To find why the components had worn to such a level, the organization would have to consider the following issues: Was the machine being used in a way it wasn't designed for? Was preventive

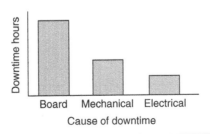

Figure A.3   Causes of downtime for Machine B.

maintenance being skipped? Was there no way to monitor component degradation on the machine? Since this line was only one of three, probing into root cause would likely be worthwhile.

HOW WOULD THEY KNOW?

An ISO 9001 surveillance audit had already been scheduled, so even though the quality manager had been in the job only a few days, she had to go ahead with it. Right away the registration auditor wrote a nonconformity for the fact that there was no evidence any internal audits had been done in the last year. That one required an immediate response!

The quality manager figured there could be only two causes: (1) no audits had been scheduled, or (2) the scheduled audits hadn't been conducted (see Figure A.4). Asking and looking for an audit schedule resulted in finding nothing (lack of a schedule was the physical cause), so she pulled the audit procedure to see what it said. It indicated that audits were to be done according to the schedule, what the qualification requirements were for the auditors, and how audits findings were to be reported. However, it did not define responsibilities or methods for creating the audit schedule (the system cause).

The quality manager quickly created an audit schedule to begin the following month, wrote up a corrective action request to initiate revision to the audit procedure, and also made a note to check into the management review procedure to see whether audits were reviewed during the process.

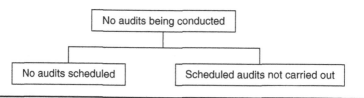

Figure A.4 Logic tree for no audits being conducted.

HOW PROFICIENT IS THAT?

A lab was required to conduct proficiency testing (PT) to ensure that test results were accurate. The researchers had seen a shift in results of one particular test a few months ago, and now the shift was back. The PT process flow consisted of receiving the sample, preparing the sample, conducting the test, interpreting the results, and reporting the results.

The same people were interpreting and reporting results as before, so the lab assumed the problem was not related to those steps (see Figure A.5). Since the sample was provided by a third-party standards lab, they decided to focus on the sample prep and testing process. Again, the same people were involved in the prepping and testing process as before, so they ruled this out as a likely cause and focused instead on equipment. Equipment involved included the reagent, the devices used to contain the sample during testing, and the test machine itself (see Figure A.6).

They first looked at test equipment records (for example, calibrations, standardizing, maintenance) and could find no possible linkages to the problem. They then looked at the lab glassware used and could find nothing to explain the problem. When they looked at the reagents they found that one, while still within the expiration date, was getting near the bottom of the container volumewise. When they looked back at when the problem had

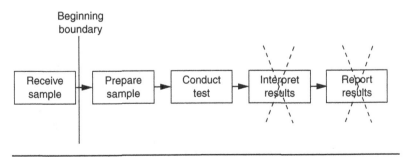

Figure A.5 PT process flow.

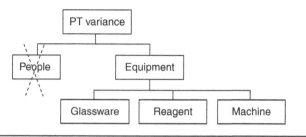

Figure A.6   PT logic tree.

previously occurred, it appeared, from the purchasing data, that the same reagent was perhaps also getting low.

Further investigation revealed that the reagent was an evaporative type that caused the concentration to become higher (albeit still within the specs). The lower the volume in the container, the more significant this effect would be. This specific test was particularly sensitive to variance in this reagent.

So they purchased a smaller bottle of the reagent and the PT results rebounded back to normal. They deduced that increasing the turnover of bottles would reduce the impact of evaporation. In order to keep the problem from recurring, they specified that only the smaller bottles would be purchased in the future.

GETTING THE SHAFT BACK

A division of a company making electromechanical assemblies has two facilities a few miles apart. One is the machining facility that produces the components, which are then transported to the other for assembly, testing, and shipment to customers.

The original problem stated by management was that too many parts were being returned from the assembly plant back to the machining facility. A Pareto analysis was conducted to look at the reasons for rejection (see Figure A.7). Since the largest problem was pinions that caused noise in the assembly, the next problem statement was "X percent of pinions are being

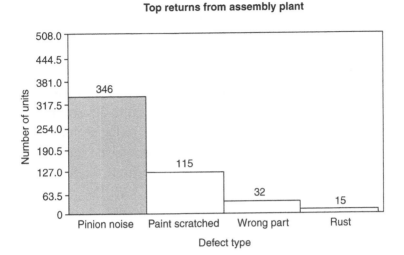

Top returns from assembly plant

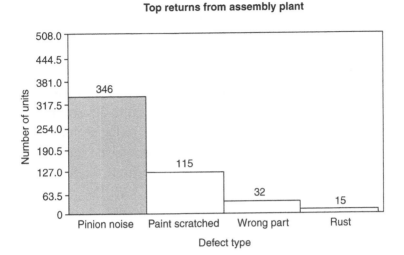

Figure A.7 Pareto of cause for returned parts.

returned from assembly due to noise." (Note: A pinion is a shaft that has teeth along a portion of its length.)

To get the project team oriented to a process focus, the facilitator asked the members to first do a high-level SIPOC analysis (see Figure A.8), which demonstrated the relationship of the machining plant to the assembly plant and the primary external supplier. The team also redefined the problem as too much runout (that is, the tooth pitch diameter was not true to

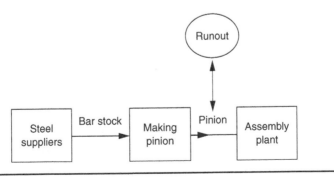

Figure A.8 SIPOC diagram for pinion problem.

the outside diameter of the pinion), since this was known to be the factor that created noise in the assembly.

The first breakthrough occurred when the team members recognized, when viewing the SIPOC, that they could visit the assembly plant and talk with the individual on the assembly line that assembled the pinion and then had to disassemble it if it was bad. This took away the anonymity of the problem, making it much more personal, with higher perceived importance.

The team then took the process step from the SIPOC and broke it down into more detail (see Figure A.9). They then brainstormed possible causes for each step:

- Bar machine not putting center in correctly

- Hobbing teeth off center

- Grinding off center

- Part warping at heat treat

- Parts damaged during transport

The team members then decided that for the next run of the pinion process they would measure the runout of every pinion (a typical batch was 30 parts) as it came off each machine.

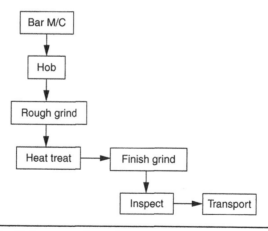

Figure A.9   Pinion manufacturing process.

Pinions were handled in a way that allowed knowing which one was which, and data were collected for each pinion at each step (see partial example in Table A.1).

The data for the 30 pinions were then put into a histogram for each step of the process. Figure A.10 shows the distribution for each step, with the curves representing the histogram turned on its side. Note that the data show that the distribution for pinion runout got much worse (more runout on average) at the rough grind process, indicating that it was causing a major change in part quality.

With this information, the team then brainstormed possible causes for the rough grinder to cause runout:

- Grinding spindle problems (for example, worn bearings)

- Collet slipping

- Collet not centered

- Collet not being used

Table A.1 Runout data collection table.

Pinion #	Runout				
	Bar M/C	**Hob**	**Rough**	**HT**	**Assembly**
1	.0003	.0004	.0012	.0011	.0013
2	.0006	.0006	.0017	.0016	.0016
3					
...					

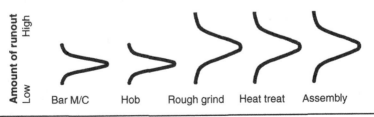

Figure A.10 Distributions of runout.

Since the collet was listed three times, they decided to look at it first. They found it in the drawer at the machine, no longer being used (the machine could be run by locating the pinion on the center stub instead). They decided to install the collet, run some parts, and see if the problem went away; it did.

So the physical cause was the collet not being used. The root cause? Since the organization had total control over both product and process design, it allowed people to make process changes (but not engineering changes) without reviewing and validating the change. So the lack of a process change procedure was rectified.

GOT IT IN THE BAG!

An organization places materials into 25-pound bags using a semiautomatic machine on which the operator loads an empty bag, hits a button, and then removes the bag when the machine indicates the bag is full. A scale is occasionally used to verify that the bag weight is correct, and it indicates when there is a problem.

A flowchart of the bagging process was done (see Figure A.11), and it was decided to increase the sampling to 100 percent inspection in order to study variation in the process. The bag weights looked random most of the time, but occasionally there was a period when several bags were heavier than normal, as shown in Figure A.12. Workers continued to monitor the process until someone noticed that the heavy bags always occurred after a break or lunch.

They surmised that the cause must be related to the preload, air feed, or bag-hanging or unloading process. They tried leaving the machine with and without combinations of empty and full bags during a break, but this had no effect. They then looked at how the preload process works, and found that when the machine was operated continuously, the preload container

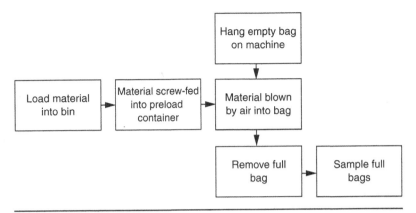

Figure A.11   Bagging process flow.

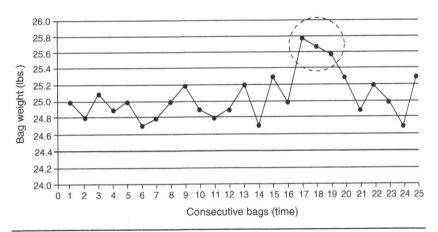

Figure A.12   Bag weights over time.

was not kept full. However, if the machine was left turned on without bagging, the container would fill up completely.

So the physical cause was related to the design of the machine, which they could not change. However, they did change the operating procedure to require the machine to be turned off when not being operated continuously, which solved the problem.

Appendix B

Root Cause Analysis Process Guides

This appendix includes several items that are useful for guiding people through the root cause analysis process or that help improve the problem-solving and corrective action processes.

GENERIC PROCESS THINKING

It's amazing how often people say, "X won't work in my organization. We're different." But after having worked with people from literally hundreds of different organizations, the author can pretty confidently say that organizations are much more alike than they are different. One of the ways this is true is that every organization carries out processes, although the cycle time and/or complexity may differ.

Since good root cause analysis requires knowing how to diagnose processes, it is then sometimes necessary to calibrate people in the organization as to how nearly anything can be viewed as a process. Figure B.1 is provided as one means, whereby several different types of organizations are listed and

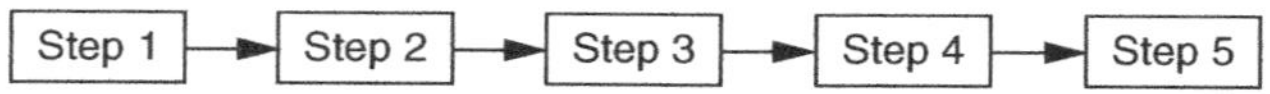

Industry/ application	Step 1	Step 2	Step 3	Step 4	Step 5	Y variable	Some X variables
Manufacturing	Receive order	Schedule order	Produce order	Package product	Ship product	Product quality	Raw materials, equipment
Distribution	Receive material	Stock	Pull	Repackage	Ship	Damage	Product type, department
Insurance	Receive claim	Identify routing	Assess claim	Pay or deny	Close	Decision accuracy	Agents, guidelines
Banking	Receive $	Deposit	Invest	Disperse	Report	Accurate report	Computer, printer
Health care	Admit	Pre-op	Operation	Post-op	Discharge	Health	Physicians, infection control
Information technology	Requirements	Design	Code	Test	Run	# System crashes	Programmers, test algorithms used
Education	Admit	Assess	Educate	Assess	Graduate	Capable	Instructor, parents, exams

Step 1 → Step 2 → Step 3 → Step 4 → Step 5

Figure B.1 Generic process thinking.

one of their core processes flowcharted. Of course, not all will have five boxes; this was simply a convenience to help show similarities.

For each process, one measure of the output (Y) of the process has been identified. Then, one or more process variables (Xs) that might affect performance of the process are also listed.

SIPOC ANALYSIS FORM

One way to help people understand their organization, their department, or their own work activity as a process is to use the Supplier-Input-Process-Output-Customer (SIPOC) model. Figure B.2 is a form that people can use to perform such an analysis.

They do this by first identifying what organization/department/process/activity they want to analyze (the process). Then they list what this process provides to someone (the outputs), followed by who that someone is (the customers). Determining how the customer might evaluate the quality of the output—what they would measure—is then listed (the outcomes).

Then the analysis moves to the left side, asking what the process must receive in order for it to be able to operate (the inputs) and who they are received from (the suppliers). How the organization would evaluate the adequacy of those inputs is then listed (the incomes).

At the bottom of the form is an opportunity to begin decomposing the process by defining the input and output boundaries, and the major steps between them. One or more of these steps can then be moved to another SIPOC analysis sheet and the process repeated.

Process/Project goal:				
Suppliers	Inputs	Process	Outputs	Customers
	Incomes		Outcomes	
Major process steps				
Process start boundary				Process end boundary

Figure B.2 SIPOC analysis form.

DATA COLLECTION AND ANALYSIS TOOLS

Throughout this book many tools and techniques have been presented that can be used to gather and/or analyze data in order to objectively evaluate possible causes.

Root cause analysis is about finding which X variable is affecting the Y variable we're concerned about. X variables can be classified into types, including entity, location, time, or parameter. Table B.1 may be useful for providing guidance on which tools to use to collect and analyze data, based on which type of X variable one believes may be affecting Y.

Examples of X Types

- Entity: Machine, people, process line, batch of something (things that would typically be counted)

Table B.1 Data collection and analysis tools.

X variable type	Tool for collecting data	Tool for analyzing data
Entity	Check sheet, generic data collection sheet	Pareto, contingency table
Location	Pictogram, check sheet	Pictogram, Pareto
Time	Generic data collection sheet, run chart	Run chart
Parameter	Run chart, generic data collection sheet	Run chart, histogram, scatter diagram
Any, but using text data	Interviews, observation of text records	Affinity diagram and interrelationship diagram, time journal or flowchart, content analysis
Any	(as above)	Is/Is-not table

- Location: Physical position within a building, on something (for example, part, person)

- Time: Hour of day, shift, day of week, month

- Parameter: Temperature, pH, viscosity, volume, age (things that are typically measured)

DO IT² ROOT CAUSE ANALYSIS GUIDE

Although the author has tried to keep the content of this book concise, there is still a lot of information one must retain if planning to use the 10-step model. Table B.2 summarizes each of the 10 steps according to what questions one is trying to ask at each step and what the output of that step is likely to be. This table will be useful for those who want to follow the model, and also for those who are responsible for coaching/facilitating the root cause analysis process.

Table B.2 DO IT² root cause analysis guide.

Step	Questions	Outputs
1. Define the problem	• What is the right problem to work on (frequency, cost, risk)? • Is it scoped to a reasonable size? • What is it, where and how much does it occur? • How does it perform over time?	• Pareto for selecting right problem • Pareto for scoping problem • Run chart showing how it performs over time • Problem statement
2. Understand the process	• What are the boundaries? • What are the major steps between the boundaries?	• Process flowchart

(Continued)

Table B.2   DO IT² root cause analysis guide. (Continued)

3. Identify possible causes	• Which is the best way to identify causes? • What changes may have been made and/or occurred in the process? • What barriers might have failed?	• List of most likely causes (flowchart, logic tree, or brainstorming)
4. Collect the data	• What data to collect (e.g., which Y data, X data)? • What sample size and method, over what time frame? • What level of accuracy and precision (e.g., # of decimal points)? • How will the data be analyzed (e.g., which tools)?	• Data collection and analysis plan • Forms and training for data collection • Data collected
5. Analyze the data	• How to slice/dice the Y data by X variables? • Have we gone deep enough into the 5 whys? • If the problem found is the physical cause, should the process root cause also be pursued?	• Charts/graphs used to analyze the data • Conclusions regarding which X variables are and/ or are not creating the problem • (Revise problem statement and return to Step 1 if needed)
6. Identify possible solutions	• What could prevent the problem?	• List of possible solutions
7. Select solution(s) to be implemented	• Which solution is best, based on economics, technical impact, time/ effort required to implement, impact on other variables, capability to sustain?	• Solutions to implement and rationale to support (e.g., decision table, benefit/cost analysis)

(Continued)

Table B.2 DO IT^2 root cause analysis guide. (Continued)

8. Implement the solution(s)	• What needs to be acquired? • What training and communications need to be done? • Where will resistance occur and how to offset it? • Who should do each item, and when?	• Implementation plan (e.g., action item list with actions, responsibilities, timing), including both technical and organizational change actions
9. Evaluate the effects	• Did the problem go away or is it less? • If it is better, is it because of the action taken? • If it isn't better, where in the 10 steps did things go wrong?	• Chart/graph/ data showing how process performance is now different from what it was before project was initiated
10. Institutionalize the change	• What actions need to be taken in order to make the change permanent (e.g., revise which procedures, job descriptions, or training materials)? • What will be done to monitor the process, and for how long, to ensure it is sustained (e.g., tracking outcomes, auditing process)? • Where else in the facility/company might this solution be useful? • What was learned during this project that could help us be more effective at future projects?	• Revised drawings, specs, procedures, etc. • Communication to other process owners, managers, facilities where the knowledge gained might be useful

DO IT² PROBLEM-SOLVING WORKSHEET

Although less detailed than Table B.2, a form such as that shown in Figure B.3 could also be useful for guiding someone through the process. At a minimum, individuals who want to

1. Define the problem	It is	It isn't
What		
Where		
When		
How much		
Problem statement		
2. Understand the process		
Boundaries	**Starts:**	**Ends:**
Major steps		
3. Identify possible causes	It could be	It couldn't be
4. Data collected		
5. Actual causes	**Physical**	**System**
Evidence to support causes		
6. Possible solutions		
7. Selected solutions		
Reason for selected solutions		
8. Implementation plan		
What		
Who		
When		
9. Results of follow-up		
Actions required		
10. Institutionalize the change		

Figure B.3 DO IT² problem solving worksheet.

improve their corrective action process should consider how providing such structure can be helpful. For example, when someone writes down what she or he believes to be the root cause, he or she must also document any supporting evidence (see Step 5 on the form), as this will force a level of thinking not often used.

CHECKLIST FOR REVIEWING THE CORRECTIVE ACTION PROCESS

Throughout this book not only has the technical process for diagnosing problems been detailed, but several additional issues have been raised that can affect how well problem solving and corrective action are carried out. The checklist in Table B.3 is provided as one means for reviewing the broader corrective action process to determine whether it is likely to produce effective results.

Table B.3 Checklist for reviewing the corrective action process.

Question to ask	Potential evaluation criteria
Are appropriate sources of information evaluated for potential corrective action?	• Product, process, and system indicators • Internal and external sources
Are the data analyzed to evaluate significance and trends?	• Pareto or pivot table analysis • Run charts or control charts
Is there a filter for evaluating whether findings are sufficient to require corrective action?	• Frequency and risk • Cost • Current number of corrective action requests in system • Business strategy/objectives
Are responsibilities clearly identified?	• Process owner • Root cause analyst

(Continued)

Table B.3   Checklist for reviewing the corrective action process. (Continued)

Are steps for problem diagnosis (root cause analysis) provided?	• More than one step • Involves process analysis • Iterative to drill down
Are appropriate tools used to support the diagnosis?	• Flowchart for process analysis • Logic tree or cause-and-effect diagram • Data analysis tools
Is the analysis taken to sufficient depth?	• Decision whether to stop at physical cause
Is there evidence to support the causes that were found?	• Data that point to the cause(s) • Data that eliminate other causes
When a barrier failed, were two diagnoses performed?	• Cause of the barrier failing • Cause of the problem itself
Are corrections and corrective actions validated as effective?	• Short-term and long-term evaluation • Supported by data for both X and Y
Is it determined whether other problems might be or were created?	• System interface analysis • Multiple follow-up metrics evaluated
Are analyses documented such that a reasonable person would agree with them?	• Shows linkage among symptoms, causes, and solutions
Is the learning shared with others?	• Used as preventive actions for similar products/processes • Policies/procedures/training revised
Is meta analysis conducted to look for higher-level causes?	• Problem categories • Cause categories
Does organizational culture support effective problem diagnosis?	• Problems are seen as learning opportunities • People are not negatively treated for system problems or honest mistakes

Appendix C
Additional Resources

In addition to the books and articles listed in the references section, the author has found the following resources useful for root cause analysis.

BOOKS

For studying the tools for collecting and analyzing data:

Brassard, M., and D. Ritter. 1994. *Memory Jogger II: A Pocket Guide of Tools for Continuous Improvement & Effective Planning*. Methuen, MA: GOAL/QPC.

For other models for root cause analysis:

Ammerman, M. 1998. *The Root Cause Analysis Handbook: A Simplified Approach to Identifying, Correcting, and Reporting Workplace Errors*. New York: Productivity Press.

Andersen, B., and T. Fagerhaug. 2006. *Root Cause Analysis: Simplified Tools and Techniques*. 2nd ed. Milwaukee, WI: ASQ Quality Press.

Gano, D. 2007. *Apollo Root Cause Analysis: A New Way of Thinking*. 3rd ed. Richland, WA: Apollonian Publications.

Latini, R., and K. Latino. 2002. *Root Cause Analysis: Improving Performance for Bottom-Line Results*. 2nd ed. New York: CRC Press.

Preuss, P. 2003. *School Leader's Guide to Root Cause Analysis: Using Data to Dissolve Problems*. Larchmont, NY: Eye on Education.

Vanden Heuvel, L., D. Lorenzo, R. Montgomery, W. Hanson, and J. Rooney. 2005. *Root Cause Analysis Handbook: A Guide to Effective Incident Investigation*. Brookfield, CT: Rothstein Associates.

WEB SITES

http://www.apqc.org
The American Productivity and Quality Center has a process classification framework that is useful for seeing organizations as structured levels of processes.

http://www.mistakeproofing.com
This Web site is a great resource for learning about and seeing many examples of mistake-proofing applications.

http://www.triz-journal.com
A resource for another view of creative thinking, based on the Russian technique known as TRIZ (pronounced "trees").

References

Buzan, T. 1996. *The Mind Map Book.* New York: Penguin Books.

Covey, S. R. 1989. *The Seven Habits of Highly Effective People: Powerful Lessons in Personal Change.* New York: Simon & Schuster.

Crossen, M. 2007. "Mr. Pareto Head." ASQ *Quality Progress* 40 (3): 10.

DeBono, E. "Six Thinking Hats," http://www.debonothinkingsystems.com/tools/6hats.htm (accessed September 28, 2008).

Dekker, S. 2006. *The Field Guide to Understanding Human Error.* Burlington, VT: Ashgate.

Gonzales, L. 2005. *Deep Survival: Who Lives, Who Dies, and Why.* New York: W.W. Norton & Company.

Groopman, J. 2007. *How Doctors Think.* Boston: Houghton Mifflin Company.

Hawkins, J. 2004. *On Intelligence.* With S. Blakeslee. New York: Henry Holt and Company.

Hubbard, D. W. 2007. *How to Measure Anything: Finding the Value of "Intangibles" in Business.* Hoboken, NJ: John Wiley & Sons.

International Organization for Standardization (ISO). 2007. *The ISO Survey of Certifications 2006.*

JCAHO (Joint Commission on Accreditation of Healthcare Organizations). 2005. *Root Cause Analysis in Health Care: Tools and Techniques.* 3rd ed. Oakbrook Terrace, IL: JCAHO.

Kepner, C. H., and B. B. Tregoe. 1981. *The New Rational Manager.* London: John Martin Publishing.

Kohn, L. T., J. M. Corrigan, and M. S. Donaldson, eds. 1999. *To Err Is Human: Building a Safer Health System.* Washington, D.C.: Institute of Medicine Committee on Quality of Health Care in America.

Loeb, J. M., and D. S. O'Leary. 2004. "The Fallacy of the Body Count: Why the Interest in Patient Safety and Why Now?" In *The Patient Safety Handbook*, ed. B. J. Youngberg and M. J. Hatlie, 83–94. Boston: Jones and Bartlett Publishers.

Lowenthal, J. 2002. *Survival Skills in Financial Services: Strategies for Turbulent Times.* New York: John Wiley & Sons.

MacDuffie, J. P. 1997. "The Road to Root Cause: Shop-Floor Problem Solving at Three Auto Assembly Plants." *Management Science* 43 (April): 479–502.

NASA Root Cause Analysis Overview. 2003. http://www.hq.nasa.gov/office/codeq/rca/rootcauseppt.pdf.

Norman, D. 1988. *The Design of Everyday Things.* New York: Doubleday.

Okes, D., and R. T. Westcott. 2001. *The Certified Quality Manager Handbook.* 2nd ed. Milwaukee, WI: ASQ Quality Press.

Plous, S. 1993. *The Psychology of Judgment and Decision Making.* New York: McGraw-Hill.

Popper, C. 1963. *Conjectures and Refutations: The Growth of Scientific Knowledge.* New York: Routledge.

Reason, J. 1990. *Human Error.* New York: Cambridge University Press.

Roam, D. 2008. *The Back of the Napkin.* New York: Penguin Books.

Rogers, E. M. 1995. *Diffusion of Innovations.* 4th ed. New York: Free Press.

Rooney, J. J., and L. N. Vanden Heuvel. 2004. "Root Cause Analysis for Beginners." ASQ *Quality Progress* 37 (July): 45–52.

Sobek II, D. K., and A. Smalley. 2008. *Understanding A3 Thinking: A Critical Component of Toyota's PDCA Management System.* Boca Raton, FL: CRC Press.

Taleb, N. N. 2007. *The Black Swan: The Impact of the Highly Improbable.* New York: Random House.

Ulrich, D., S. Kerr, and R. Ashkenas. 2002. *The GE Workout: How to Implement GE's Revolutionary Method for Busting Bureaucracy & Attacking Organizational Problems.* New York: McGraw-Hill.

U.S. Department of Energy Office of Environment, Safety and Health. 2003. *Occurrence Reporting Causal Analysis Guide* DOE G 231.1-2.

U.S. Department of Veterans Affairs, National Center for Patient Safety. http://www.va.gov/ncps/CogAids/RCA/index.html# (accessed September 29, 2008).

Vroom, V. H., and A. G. Jago. 1976. *Leadership and Decision-Making.* Pittsburgh: University of Pittsburgh Press.

Willingham, R. 1999. *The People Principle.* New York: St. Martin's Press.

Index

S

sample size, data and, 74
sampling techniques, 74–75
scale up or scale down technique, 100
scatter diagrams, 92–94, 94*f*
scoping the problem, 30
security, data and, 82
sensory data, 68
seven Ms category, in cause-and-
  effect diagrams, 58
Shewhart, Walter, 7
Simon, Herbert, 120
SIPOC (Supplier-Input-Process-
  Output-Customer)
  diagram, 44, 44*f*
  form, 163, 164
Six Sigma DMAIC model, 6–7
six thinking hats methodology, 110
slips, 137
solutions
  evaluating effects of, 115–116
  for human errors, 137–138
  identifying possible, 99–106
    benchmarking, 104–105
    creativity techniques for,
      100–104
    mistake-proofing for, 104
    precautions for, 105–106
    TRIZ/ARIZ, 105
  implementing, 113–115
  selecting, for implementation,
    106–111
    criteria for, 107–108
    decision making for, 107
    issues in, 110–111
    tools for, 108–110
standard logic trees, 57
standard process flowcharts, 39, 40*f*
  drilling down and, 47
stratified sampling, 75
structured brainstorming, 59

structured sampling, 74
summaries, data analysis
  cause analysis tables, 96, 97*t*
  is/is-not tables, 96, 96*t*
  swim lanes flowcharts, 39, 41*f*
  symbols, flowchart, 39, 41*f*
symptoms, problem, 13–14
system causes, 14–15

T

10-step model, of problem-solving.
  See DO IT² model
text data, 68
thinking
  critical, 145
  as process, 145*f*
thought experiments, 69
time frame, data and, 74
time-oriented graphs, 31–32
time requirements, for root cause
  analysis, 131–132
tools
  for high-frequency data, 86–94
  for low-frequency data, 84–86
  for selecting solutions, 108–110
trainers, 127
TRIZ, 105

U

unstructured brainstorming, 59

V

validity, data and, 75
variation, analyzing, 97

W

what would X do (WWXD)?,
  101–102
why-why diagrams. *See* logic trees
worksites, for root cause analysis, 131